UNDERSTANDING ENERGY

PHYSICS
WORKSHOP-1

SEYMOUR ROSEN

 Globe Book Company, Inc.
New York/Cleveland/Toronto

THE AUTHOR

SEYMOUR ROSEN received his B.A. and M.S. degrees from Brooklyn College. He teaches science at the Edward B. Shallow Junior High School in Brooklyn.

Mr. Rosen participated in a teacher-training program for the development of science curriculum for the New York City Board of Education.

Editor: Lansing P. Wagner
Project Coordination: Dimensions & Directions, Ltd.

PHOTO AND ILLUSTRATION CREDITS:

Aim Opener Art: Marion Krupp
Cover: Edison Electric Institute
Technical Art: Vantage Art, Inc.

AT&T: 156 (left)
Bethlehem Steel: 146 (bottom)
Canadian Consulate General: 124 (left)
Coca Cola: 156 (center)
Cunard Lines: 146 (top left)
De Wys Inc.: 38
Energy R & D: 48
General Motors: 146 (top right)
National Oceanographic & Atmospheric Adm: 8 (left)
NY Public Library: 8 (left)
Salt River Project: 36, 156 (right)
United Nations: 32, 130
UPI: 90
Westinghouse: 124 (right)

Second Edition 1987

ISBN: 0-87065-953-7

PRINTED IN THE UNITED STATES OF AMERICA
9   10   11   12   13   14

CONTENTS

Keeping Up With Science

BEFORE YOU BEGIN . . .

You are about to take a fabulous trip. On much of your trip you'll be exploring things you know something about. But you will be looking at them in a new way.

In this book you'll learn about things you see every day: magnets, compasses, and motors, for instance. You will learn how they are made and how they work. You'll learn about things that may be new to you, too!

On this guided tour you will also discover how a thermometer and refrigerator work and how heat from the sun reaches the earth. You'll learn how to make electricity, too!

Your guide book is set up in a special way. Each stopover, or Aim, begins with the things you'll need to know. This is followed by a series of exercises. Take your time on these. And look back to the Aim page when you're not sure of an answer. There will be experiments along the way—and a few surprises, too!

So get ready. Your trip is about to begin. Have a good time . . . and, oh yes, don't forget to write!

WHAT IS STATIC ELECTRICITY?

1

matter: anything that has weight and takes up space

atom: the smallest part of matter that has matter's characteristics; an atom is so small you cannot see it

neutral: not taking sides; having no electrical charge

friction: rubbing

static: not moving

AIM 1 | What is static electricity?

Did you ever walk across a carpet, touch someone, and get a shock? That shock is caused by *static electricity* [STAT ik i leck TRISS it ee]. "Static" means not moving. Static electricity is electricity that is not moving in a path. What causes static electricity?

To understand what causes static electricity, you have to know about the *atom*. Scientists have learned that all matter is made up of tiny parts called atoms. Each atom has *charges* of electrical energy. There are two kinds of charges. There are *positive* [plus or +] charges. There are *negative* [minus or −] charges. An atom has both positive and negative charges.

Usually, an atom has the same number of positive charges as it has negative charges. Then the charges are *balanced*. The atom is *neutral* [NEW trul]. The positive and negative charges balance each other out. Then the whole atom has no charge.

Sometimes, the positive and negative charges of an atom are not equal. Then the atom is not neutral. The atom has a positive charge if it has more positive charges. The atom has a negative charge if it has more negative charges. *Matter that has charged atoms has static electricity.*

When some kinds of matter rub together, you also get static electricity. Rubbing is also known as *friction* [FRICK shun]. Sometimes static electricity is called *friction electricity.*

Static electricity is *not* the kind of electricity that we use for light bulbs, toasters, and appliances.

PLUS AND MINUS CHARGES

Charged matter may have a plus (+) charge or a minus (−) charge.

■ *Opposite* charges *attract.*

■ A *plus* or *minus* charge
and
a *neutral* charge *also* attract.

■ *Same* charges *repel.*

Four of these pairs will attract. Two pairs will repel.

Which pairs will attract?

Which pairs will repel?

Write your answers below.

+ and +
+ and −
− and −
− and +
neutral and +
neutral and −

ATTRACT

REPEL

_____   _____

_____   _____

_____

A.

The word "electricity" comes from the Greek word meaning "amber."

Amber is hardened tree sap.

Early Greeks experimented with amber. They rubbed amber against fur or cloth. This caused a slight spark and a "crackling" sound. After the amber was rubbed, it was able to pick up feathers or thin wood chips.

EXPERIMENTING WITH STATIC ELECTRICITY

First do step **1**. Then do step **2**. Answer the questions next to each step.

A.

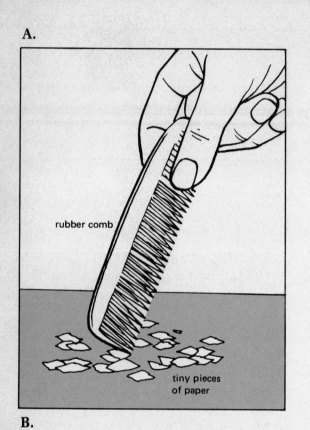

rubber comb

tiny pieces
of paper

B.

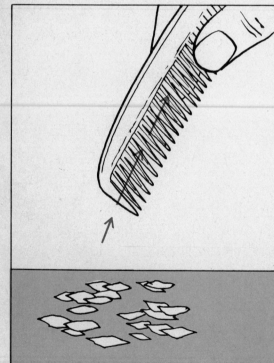

STEP 1

1. Hold a rubber comb on a few tiny pieces of paper. Then lift the comb.

a) The comb _____
   does, does not
   pick up the paper.

b) The comb _____
   charged.   is, is not

c) The paper _____
   charged.   is, is not

d) This shows that objects with *no* charge _____
   do, do not
   attract each other.

C.

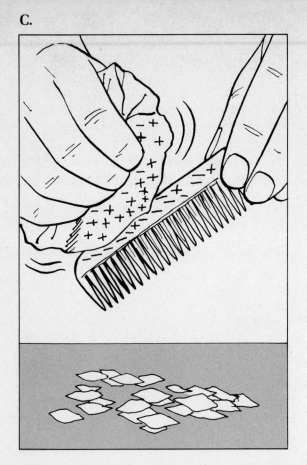

2. Rub the comb with a piece of cloth or fur. [Combing your hair may also do the job.] This rubbing causes minus charges to move from the cloth to the comb.

Then hold the comb on the paper. Lift the comb.

a) The comb _____
      does, does not

pick up the paper.

b) The comb _____
      has, has not

become charged.

c) The comb now
   a) has a plus charge.
   b) has a minus charge.
   c) is neutral.

d) The paper has
   a) has a plus charge.
   b) has a minus charge.
   c) is neutral.

e) This shows that a charged object

_____ attract a neu-
      does, does not

tral object.

D.

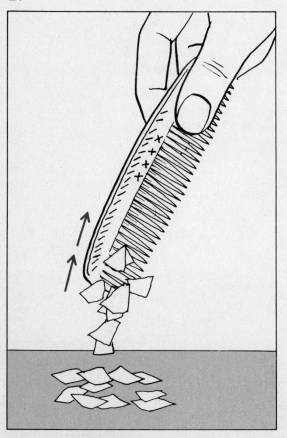

LIGHTNING

Clouds can build strong static electricity. Scientists believe that static electricity causes *lightning*.

Lightning is very dangerous. In the United States alone, lightning kills nearly 400 people every year. About 1,500 more are injured.

Every house should have a *lightning rod*. The lightning hits the lightning rod instead of the house.

The electricity then travels through a wire into the ground. No one gets hurt.

Lightning Safety Rules

During a lightning storm . . .

1. DON'T run onto an open field.

2. DON'T stay under a tree.

3. DO stay indoors or find a place indoors.

4. If you are in a car during a lightning storm, DO stay there. [Can you figure out why?]

5. If you are swimming, DO get out of the water.

WHAT DOES THE PICTURE SHOW?

Look at the picture. Then answer the questions.

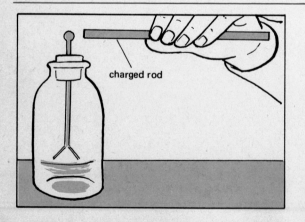

charged rod

An *electroscope* is a simple instrument. It tells us if an object has static electricity.

If you hold a charged object near the tip of an electroscope, the leaves move apart.

The leaves move apart because they

have _____ charges.
    same, opposite

MULTIPLE CHOICE

On the space on the right, write the letter that best completes each sentence.

1. An atom has
   a) only plus charges.
   b) only minus charges.
   c) plus and minus charges.

   1. _____

2. Usually, an atom has
   a) the same number of plus and minus charges.
   b) more plus charges than minus charges.
   c) more minus charges than plus charges.

   2. _____

3. "Neutral" charge means
   a) plus charge.
   b) no charge.
   c) minus charge.

   3. _____

4. Usually, an atom is
   a) charged.
   b) not charged.

   4. _____

5. Charged matter has
   a) no electricity.
   b) moving electricity.
   c) static electricity.

   5. _____

6. Static electricity
   a) moves in a path.
   b) does not move in a path.
   c) is neutral.

   6. _____

7. To make 100 minus charges neutral, you need
   a) 50 minus charges and 50 plus charges.
   b) 100 minus charges.
   c) 100 plus charges.

   7. _____

8. *Same* charges
   a) attract.
   b) repel.
   c) do not attract or repel.

   8. _____

9. *Opposite* charges
   a) attract.
   b) repel.
   c) do not attract or repel.

   9. _____

10. Static electricity can come from
    a) batteries.
    b) rubbing.
    c) ancient Greece.

    10. _____

MATCHING Match the two lists. Write the correct letter on the line next to each number.

1. _____ opposite charges   **a)** means "not moving"

2. _____ neutral   **b)** repel

3. _____ rubbing   **c)** attract

4. _____ static   **d)** charges are balanced

5. _____ same charges   **e)** can cause static electricity

REACHING OUT Benjamin Franklin was a famous American. He invented many useful things.

Franklin did many experiments with electricity. It is said that during one experiment he flew a kite during a thunderstorm.

1. Why should you not do this? _____

_____

2. What can a kite act as? _____

_____

WHAT IS CURRENT ELECTRICITY?

2

circuit: a path that ends at the same point where it starts

generator: machine that makes electricity

AIM 2 | What is current electricity?

Think of all the ways you use electricity each day. You awake to an alarm clock or radio, turn on an electric light, use an electric toothbrush, or make toast. You watch television, listen to records, use air conditioners. Just think about lights. Almost every place you go you find electrical lighting.

About one hundred years ago, there was no electricity in homes, schools, factories, and offices. Try to imagine your life without electricity!

The electricity that works all your electrical appliances is called *current electricity*. A current is a flow of water. Current electricity is a flow of *electrons* [i LECK tronz]. Electrons are the parts of the atom that have a negative charge. There is another part of the atom that has a positive charge.

Electrons move along a path called a *circuit* [SIR cut]. While the electrons are moving, the circuit is *complete*. If the electrons stop moving, the circuit is *incomplete* and the electricity stops.

Some of our electricity comes from batteries. Small batteries like those used for flashlights are called *dry cells*. Most of our electricity comes from machines called *generators* [JEN uh ray terz].

Each year, the world uses more and more electricity. More and more generators are needed.

SOME COMMON ELECTRICAL SYMBOLS

A.

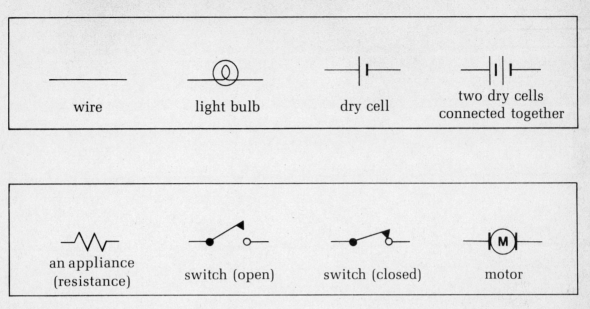

wire   light bulb   dry cell   two dry cells connected together

an appliance (resistance)   switch (open)   switch (closed)   motor

B.

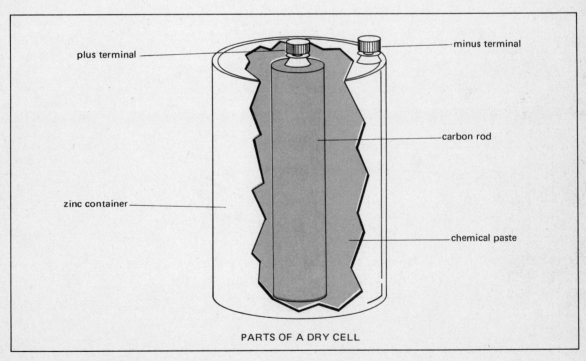

PARTS OF A DRY CELL

PARTS OF A DRY CELL

A dry cell *changes chemical energy to electric energy.*

Dry cells come in many different sizes and strengths.

WHAT DO THE PICTURES SHOW?

Look at each picture. Then answer the questions.

Anything that works with electricity is called an electrical *device*.

We call some electrical devices, *appliances*. Electricians call them *loads*.

C.

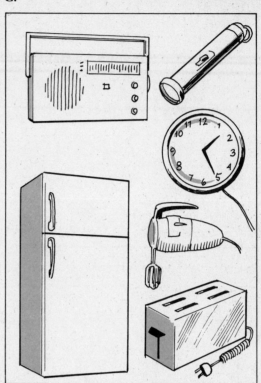

1. Figure **C** shows some electrical devices. How many can you name?

_____

_____

_____

_____

2. How many other electrical devices can you name?

_____

_____

_____

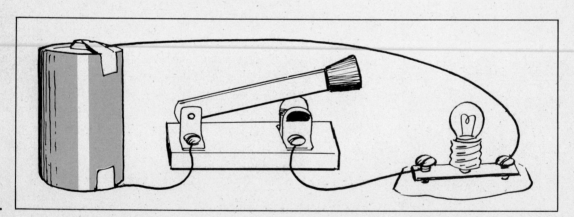

D.

1. Is this circuit complete or incomplete? _____

2. Are electrons moving? _____

3. Does the bulb light up? _____

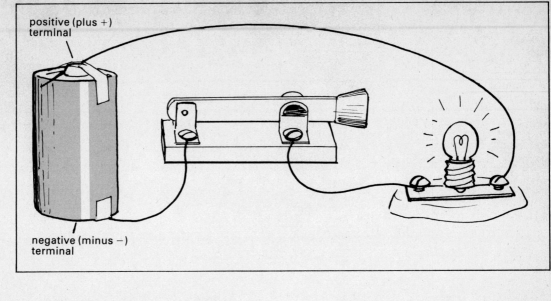

positive (plus +) terminal

negative (minus −) terminal

E.

4. Is this circuit complete or incomplete? _____

5. Are electrons moving? _____

6. Does the bulb light up? _____

7. Electricity flows *from minus to plus*. Draw arrows near the wires, the switch, and battery to show this path.

COMPLETING SENTENCES

Complete the sentences with the choices below.

complete   minus   plus
generators   move along a path   circuit
incomplete   toaster   do not move along a path

1. In *static* electricity, electrons _____.

2. In *current* electricity, electrons _____.

3. The path along which electrons move is called a _____.

4. Electrons do *not* move in an _____ circuit.

5. Electrons *do* flow in a _____ circuit.

6. Electrons leave a dry cell through the _____ terminal.

7. Electrons return to a dry cell through the _____ terminal.

8. Large amounts of electricity are made by _____.

9. An example of an electrical appliance is a _____.

CAN YOU IDENTIFY THESE ELECTRICAL SYMBOLS?

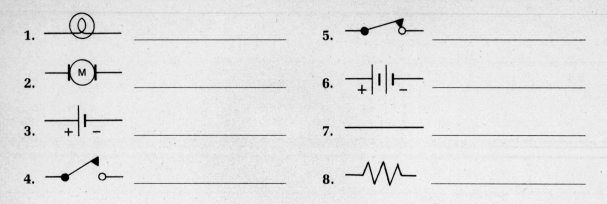

1. _____

2. _____

3. _____

4. _____

5. _____

6. _____

7. _____

8. _____

NOW LET'S DRAW!

Draw these electrical symbols. [But first cover the top of this page.]

1. one dry cell	
2. two dry cells connected together	
3. wire	
4. light bulb	
5. motor	
6. open switch	
7. closed switch	
8. an appliance (resistance)	

MATCHING   Match the two lists. Write the correct letter on the line next to each number.

1. _____ flow of electrons		a)	where electrons leave
2. _____ circuit		b)	path for moving electron
3. _____ minus terminal		c)	an electrical device
4. _____ plus terminal		d)	current electricity
5. _____ light bulb		e)	where electrons return

TRUE OR FALSE   Write T on the line next to the number if the sentence is true. Write F if the sentence is false.

1. _____ Current electricity comes from a flow of electrons.

2. _____ Static electricity lights our homes.

3. _____ Most of our electricity comes from generators.

4. _____ The path that current electricity follows is called a circus.

5. _____ Electrons leave a battery from the plus terminal.

6. _____ Electrons return to a battery through the plus terminal.

7. _____ The inside of a battery is filled with zinc.

8. _____ Batteries give static electricity.

9. _____ Generators make current electricity.

10. _____ Electrons stop moving in an incomplete circuit.

THROW ONE OUT   In each of the following sets of terms, one of the terms does *not* belong. Circle that term.

1. current electricity   moving electrons   static electricity

2. static electricity   current electricity   electrons not moving

3. complete circuit   incomplete circuit   bulb lights up

4. complete circuit   incomplete circuit   bulb does not light up

5. bicycle   flashlight   electrical device

1. NUTRECR _____

2. TIRCCUI _____

3. TARBETY _____

4. REMLATIN _____

5. CELOTERN _____

REACHING OUT Why don't we get most of our electricity from batteries?

_____

_____

_____

_____

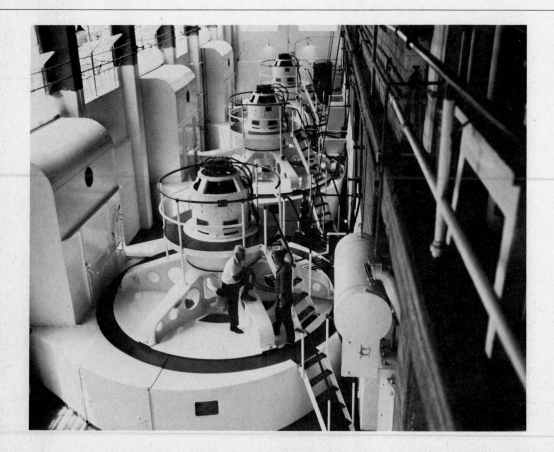

WHAT IS A SERIES CIRCUIT?

3

series circuit: an electrical hook-up in which the current has only one path

AIM 3 | What is a series circuit?

How many light bulbs are there in your home? How many other electrical devices do you have?

Must they *all* be working if you want to use just one?

Do they *all* stop working if you shut off just one?

Of course not! Homes are not wired that way. But there are electrical hook-ups that work so that all electrical devices on the circuit are either on or off. This kind of electrical hook-up is called a *series circuit*.

There are two important things to remember about a series circuit:

1. *Electrons have only one path to follow* in a series circuit. Each electrical device is connected along this one path. Because of that, the electricity cannot go to just one device. It must move through *all*.

    If you turn off any electrical device, you will turn them all off. If you turn that device back on, you will turn on all the devices.

2. The electrical devices, or appliances, share the electrical pressure in a series circuit. If you add electrical appliances, each one gets less electrical pressure. For example, suppose you have light bulbs along a series circuit. Then you add more bulbs. What would happen? Each bulb would give off less light.

Why bother with series circuits? They don't make sense for homes, schools, or factories! But there are special uses for series circuits. Parts of computers, radios, and television sets are wired in series. Parts of space rockets are too!

A TYPICAL SERIES CONNECTION

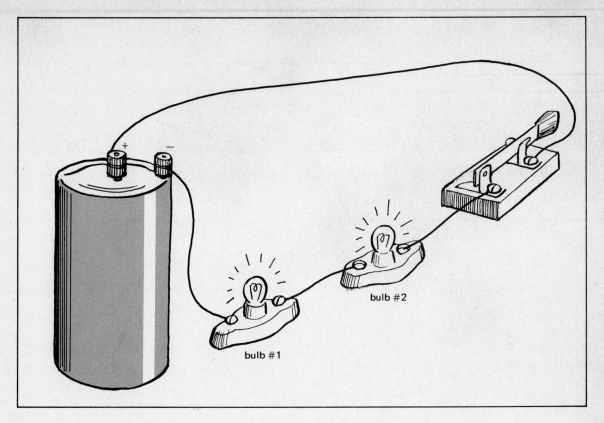

bulb #2

bulb #1

1. Trace the path of the electrons in this series circuit. (Draw in arrows along the circuit.)

2. In this circuit, the electricity has _____ paths to follow.
   <u>one, two</u>

3. This circuit is _____.
   <u>complete, incomplete</u>

4. Where does the electricity have to go before it reaches bulb #2? _____

5. If bulb #1 were to go out, bulb #2 would _____.
   <u>stay lit, go out</u>

6. If bulb #2 were to go out, bulb #1 would _____.
   <u>stay lit, go out</u>

7. In this circuit, each bulb _____ getting the full voltage.
   <u>is, is not</u>

8. If more bulbs were added to this circuit, each bulb would give off _____ light.
   <u>more, less</u>

9. If this circuit had only one bulb, it would give off _____ light.
   <u>more, less</u>

Complete the sentences with the choices below.

go off   moving electrons   switched on
less   series   are not
one   share

1. The circuit you are learning about in this Aim is the _____ circuit.

2. In a series circuit, electrons have only _____ path to follow.

3. In a series circuit, when one appliance is shut off, all other appliances

    _____.

4. In a series circuit, when one appliance is switched on, *all* other appliances must

    be _____.

5. In a series circuit, the appliances _____ the electrical pressure.

6. In a series circuit, when you add more appliances, each appliance gets

    _____ power.

7. Homes, factories, and schools _____ wired in series.

8. Current electricity comes from _____.

MATCHING Match the two lists. Write the correct letter on the line next to
each number.

1. _____ charged atoms that are   **a)** only one path for electrons to
            not moving   move

2. _____ moving electrons   **b)** ending point of a circuit

3. _____ series circuits   **c)** static electricity

4. _____ minus terminal   **d)** starting point of a circuit

5. _____ plus terminal   **e)** current electricity

WHAT DO THE PICTURES SHOW?

Look at each picture. Then answer the questions.

Quiet! Electrical Engineer at work!

Four series circuits are shown below. Use arrows to show the path of the electricity in each one.

Remember: A series circuit has *only one* path for the electrons to follow.

A.

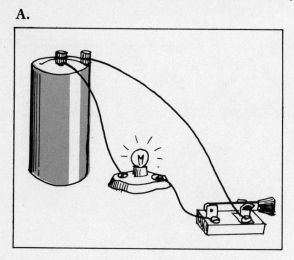

How many paths are there in this

circuit ? _____

B.

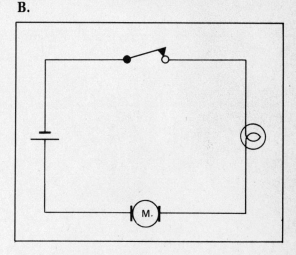

How many paths are there in this

circuit ? _____

C.

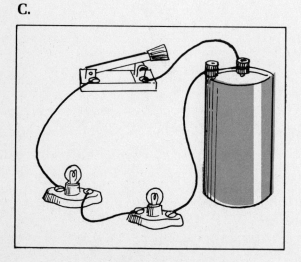

How many paths are there in this

circuit ? _____

D.

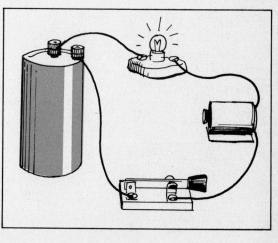

How many paths are there in this

circuit ? _____

COMPLETE
THE CHART
Use electrical *symbols* to draw these series circuits.

1. one dry cell
    one open switch
    two motors

2. two dry cells
    one closed switch
    three light bulbs

3. one dry cell
    no switch
    three loads (your choices)

4. two dry cells
    one open switch
    one motor
    two light bulbs

WHAT IS A PARALLEL CIRCUIT?

4

1½ VOLTS

parallel circuit: an electrical hook-up in which the current has *more* than one path

AIM 4 | What is a parallel circuit?

You walk into your home and switch on the TV. You switch on *only* the TV. You don't have to switch on the toaster and broiler, the hair dryer and radio—You don't have to because your home is *not* wired in series. Your home is wired in *parallel*.

There are two important facts you should know about parallel circuits:

1. In a parallel circuit, *the electrons have more than one path to follow. Each appliance has its own path.* This lets you use or shut off only one appliance at a time.
2. In a parallel circuit, *the appliances do not share the electrical pressure.* Each appliance gets the full voltage it needs. Adding more loads does *not* weaken the force. Each load still works with full power. For example, adding more bulbs to a parallel circuit does not make each bulb give off less light.

Parallel circuits make sense for use in homes, schools, and factories.

A TYPICAL PARALLEL CONNECTION

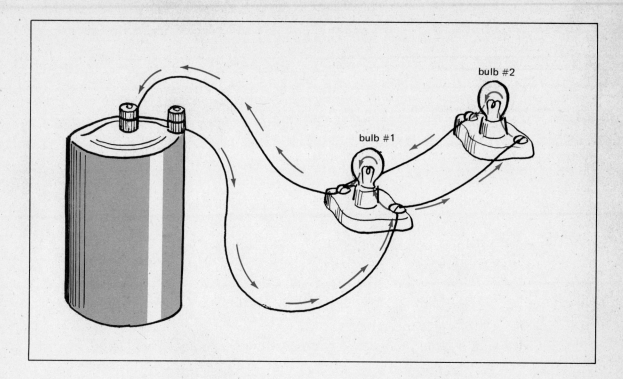

Look at this diagram. Then answer the questions.

1. How many bulbs are in this parallel circuit? _____

2. How many paths does the electricity have to follow? _____ Follow the paths that are shown with your pencil.

3. Is this circuit complete or incomplete? _____

4. Do the bulbs light up? _____

5. Does the electricity have to pass through bulb #1 for bulb #2 to light up? _____

6. If bulb #2 were to blow out, bulb #1 would _____.

stay lit, go out

7. If bulb #1 were to blow out, bulb #2 would _____.

stay lit, go out

8. If a *third* bulb were added, bulbs #1 and #2 would

   _____.

give off less light, give off the same amount of light

9. The bulbs in this circuit _____ share the electrical pressure.

do, do not

10. Your home is wired _____.

in parallel, in series

Choose the correct word or term for each statement. Write your choice in the space.

1. Homes, schools and factories, _____ wired in series.
   are, are not

2. This school is wired in _____ .
   parallel, series

3. In a *series* circuit, electricity has _____ path to follow.
   one, more than one

4. In a *parallel* circuit, electricity has _____ path to follow.
   one, more than one

5. In a *series* circuit, when one bulb goes out, the other bulbs _____ .
   stay lit, go off

6. In a *parallel* circuit, when one bulb shuts off, the other bulbs _____ .
   stay lit, go off

7. An extra bulb is added to a series circuit. The other bulbs now give off

   _____ .
   less light, the same amount of light

8. An extra bulb is added to a parallel circuit. The other bulbs now give off

   _____ .
   less light, the same amount of light

9. In a *parallel* circuit, you _____ use or shut off one appliance at a time.
   can, cannot

10. In a *series* circuit, you _____ use or shut off one appliance at a time.
    can, cannot

MATCHING Match the two lists. Write the correct letter on the line next to each number.

1. _____ parallel circuit

2. _____ series circuit

3. _____ another bulb added to a parallel circuit

4. _____ another bulb added to a series circuit

a) does not change amount of light each bulb gives

b) loads work together

c) loads work one at a time

d) does change amount of light each bulb gives

WORKING WITH CIRCUITS

Look at each circuit. Then answer the questions next to it.

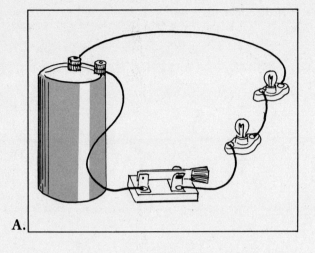

A.

(Note: *Do not count a switch as a load.*)

1. What kind of circuit is this? _____

   _____

2. How many paths do the electrons have to follow? _____

3. How many loads does this circuit have? _____

4. Is the circuit complete or incomplete? _____

5. Are the loads working? _____

6. If one bulb were to blow out, the other bulb would _____
   <u>stay lit, shut off</u>

7. Adding another bulb would make the other two give off

   _____ .
   <u>less light, the same amount of light</u>

8. This _____ a good way to wire a home.
   <u>is, is not</u>

B.

1. What kind of circuit is this? _____

2. How many loads does this circuit have? _____

3. How many paths do the electrons have to follow? _____

4. Is the circuit complete or incomplete? _____

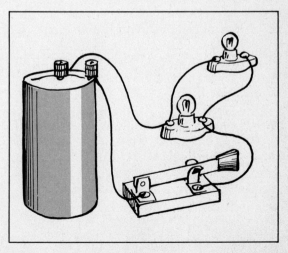

5. Are the loads working? _____

6. If one bulb were to go off, the other bulb would give off

   _____.
   more light, the same amount of light

7. Adding another bulb, would make each bulb give off _____.
   less light, the same amount of light

8. Is this a good way to wire a home? _____

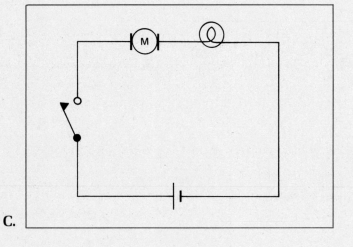

C.

1. What kind of circuit is this? _____
   parallel, series

2. How many paths do the electrons have to follow? _____

3. How many loads does this circuit have? _____

   Name them. _____ _____

4. Is the circuit complete or incomplete? _____

5. Are the loads working? _____

6. Is your home wired this way? _____

28

1. What kind of circuit is this?

_____
parallel, series

2. How many paths do the electrons have to follow? _____

3. How many loads does this circuit have? _____

Name them. _____

_____

D.

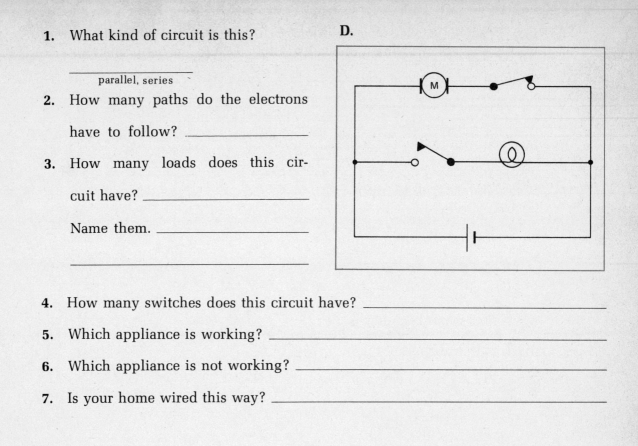

4. How many switches does this circuit have? _____

5. Which appliance is working? _____

6. Which appliance is not working? _____

7. Is your home wired this way? _____

E.

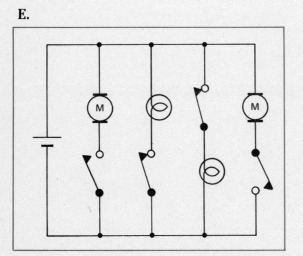

1. What kind of circuit is this?

_____

2. How many paths do the electrons have to follow? _____

3. How many loads does this circuit have? _____

Name them. _____

_____

4. How many switches does this circuit have? _____

5. Which loads are working? _____

_____

6. Which loads are not working? _____

_____

7. Is your school wired this way? _____

CHECK THE CIRCUIT

Each phrase below describes either a parallel circuit or a series circuit. Which one is it? Put a check (√) in the proper box.

		Parallel Circuit	Series Circuit
1.	only one path for the electricity to follow		
2.	more than one path for the electricity to follow		
3.	loads work or shut off one at a time		
4.	all loads are on or all loads are off		
5.	appliances share the voltage		
6.	appliances do not share the voltage		
7.	good way to wire a home		
8.	not a good way to wire homes		
9.	an extra bulb makes the others less bright		
10.	an extra bulb does not change the brightness of the others		

THROW ONE OUT

In each of the following sets of terms, one of the terms does *not* belong. Circle that term.

1. parallel circuit   loads must work together   wiring in this school

2. series circuit   loads must work together   wiring in this school

3. electrical symbol   ♡   —◯—   —┤├—

4. switch open   complete circuit   switch closed

5. generator   switch   battery

REVIEWING ELECTRICAL SYMBOLS

Draw the following electrical symbols.

1.	open switch	
2.	closed switch	
3.	one dry cell	
4.	two dry cells	
5.	wire	
6.	motor	
7.	light bulb	

TRUE OR FALSE Write T on the line next to the number if the sentence is true. Write F if the sentence is false.

1. _____ A dry cell gives static electricity.

2. _____ Static electricity lights our homes.

3. _____ Static electricity causes lightning.

4. _____ A safe place to stay during a lightning storm is under a tree.

5. _____ Electricity is useful.

6. _____ Electricity can be dangerous.

7. _____ This school is wired in parallel.

8. _____ Your home is wired in series.

9. _____ A parallel circuit lets you use or shut off one appliance at a time.

10. _____ Appliances wired in parallel share the electrical pressure.

Draw these circuits. Use electrical *symbols*.

1. *complete series circuit*
- one battery
- one switch
- three bulbs

2. *complete parallel circuit*
- one battery
- one switch
- three motors

3. *incomplete parallel circuit*
- two batteries
- two switches
- one bulb, one motor

WHAT IS ELECTRICAL RESISTANCE?

5

resist: to work against

nichrome: a metal that resists electricity very much

molecule: two or more atoms linked up

AIM 5 | What is electrical resistance?

Imagine that you are walking against a strong wind. It isn't easy to walk. The wind is slowing you down. It is trying to stop you. We say the wind *resists* your movement.

Everything that moves meets some kind of *resistance*. Even electricity meets resistance.

Electric wire resists the flow of electrons. It tries to stop the electrons. The resistance makes the atoms and molecules rub together. This rubbing, or friction, builds heat. The greater the resistance, the greater the heat.

Electrical resistance can be slight—or very great—or in-between. Resistance depends mainly on three things. They are: *wire length*, *wire thickness*, and *the kind of metal* the wire is made of.

LENGTH OF WIRE Long wires resist electricity more than short wires do. The longer the wire, the more resistance.

THICKNESS OF WIRE Thin wires resist electricity more than thick wires do. The thinner the wire, the greater the resistance.

KIND OF METAL Some metals resist electricity more than others. Silver resists electricity the least. Copper resists electricity less than most metals. Metals that offer little resistance are good for electrical wiring. Most electrical wiring is made of copper.

Nichrome [NIE krome] is made of nickel and chromium. Nichrome offers great resistance to electricity. Metals that offer great resistance are good for producing heat. They can be used in toasters and electric irons.

RESISTANCE AND WIRE THICKNESS

Two wires A and B are shown below. They are the same length.

How are they different?

Now fill in the blanks below, using the letters A and B, depending on the wire that gives the correct answer.

A

B

1. Electrons have *more* room to move along wire _____.

2. Electrons have *less* room to move along wire _____.

3. Electrons rub *more* along wire _____.

4. Electrons rub *less* along wire _____.

5. Which wire resists the electrons *more*? _____

6. Which wire resists the electrons *less*? _____

7. There is *more* friction along wire _____.

8. There is *less* friction along wire _____.

9. Which wire stays *cooler*? _____

10. Which wire becomes *warmer*? _____

Conclusion: Thin wire resists electricity _____ than thick wire.
more, less

RESISTANCE AND WIRE LENGTH

Two wires C and D are shown below. They are both the same thickness.

How are they different?

Now fill in the blanks below, using the letters C and D, depending on the wire that gives the correct answer.

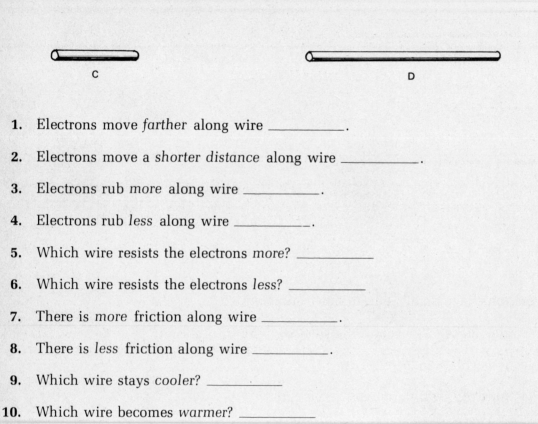

C   D

1. Electrons move *farther* along wire _____.

2. Electrons move a *shorter distance* along wire _____.

3. Electrons rub *more* along wire _____.

4. Electrons rub *less* along wire _____.

5. Which wire resists the electrons *more*? _____

6. Which wire resists the electrons *less*? _____

7. There is *more* friction along wire _____.

8. There is *less* friction along wire _____.

9. Which wire stays *cooler*? _____

10. Which wire becomes *warmer*? _____

CONCLUSION:

Long wire resists electricity _____
than short wire.   more, less

36

Choose the correct word or term for each statement. Write your choice in the space.

1. To "resist" means to _____.
    help, try to stop

2. Electrical resistance is caused by _____.
   friction, switches

3. Friction comes from _____.
   wires, rubbing

4. Friction produces _____.
   electrons, heat

5. More friction means _____ heat.
   more, less

6. Less friction means _____ heat.
   more, less

7. Long wire resists electricity _____ than short wire.
   more, less

8. Thick wire resists electricity _____ than thin wire.
   more, less

9. Nichrome is a _____ resistance wire.
   high, low

10. Copper is a _____ resistance wire.
    high, low

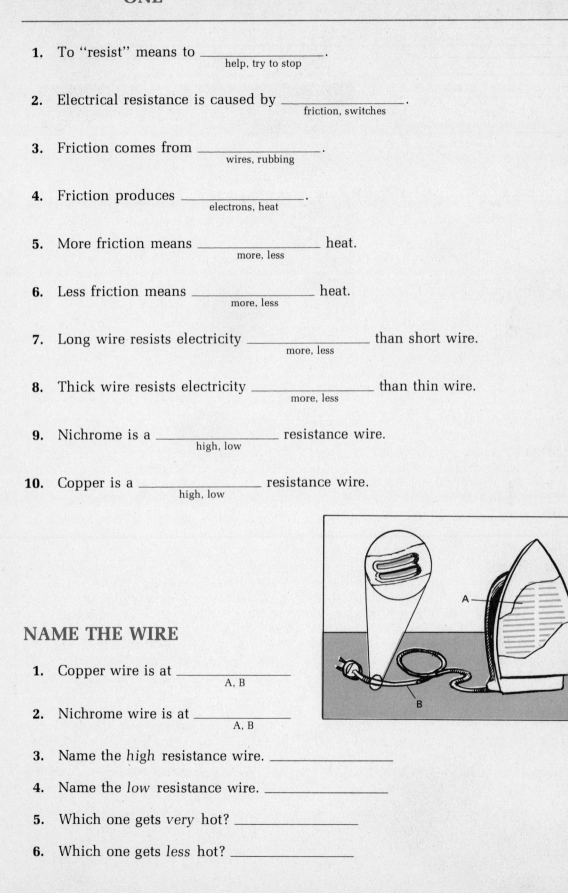

NAME THE WIRE

1. Copper wire is at _____
   A, B

2. Nichrome wire is at _____
   A, B

3. Name the *high* resistance wire. _____

4. Name the *low* resistance wire. _____

5. Which one gets *very* hot? _____

6. Which one gets *less* hot? _____

ELECTRICITY WITH NO RESISTANCE

In 1911, Dutch physicist H.K. Onnes performed an experiment. He cooled mercury to 452 degrees below zero on the Fahrenheit scale (−268.88°C). That's nearly the coldest temperature possible. Onnes then sent an electric current through the supercooled mercury. He discovered that the mercury had lost all its resistance to electrical current. Since that time, scientists have tried to find out why this happens.

We know that all atoms vibrate. We also know that removing heat slows down the vibrations. Physicists have discovered that at extremely low temperatures the vibration speed of supercooled mercury atoms is timed perfectly with passing waves of electrons. Whenever a wave of electrons (electricity) passes a group of slowed-down, supercooled atoms, the vibrating atoms move *away* from the electrons. In other words, the atoms do not get in the way of the electrons. (It is like jumping rope. The feet miss the rope—the electricity misses the atoms.) When this happens, electrical resistance disappears.

The ability of certain ultracold substances to conduct electricity without resistance is called *superconductivity*. Until recently, superconductivity was only a scientific curiosity. Scientists believed this property had great potential. But they were unable to find ways of putting it to use until recently.

The main problem was to keep the object extremely cold. This is now possible because helium gas becomes a liquid when heat is removed from it. It condenses into a liquid at −268.88°C; it does not freeze (become a solid). A constant flow of liquid helium maintains the supercold temperature. Other problems have also been solved. Superconductivity is nearly ready to serve society. But how?

Superconductivity can produce more electrical power with much less fuel. For this reason it can save energy and a great deal of money. A generator with a supercold rotor can produce *twice* as much electricity as a standard generator *twice* its size.

The first superconducting generator in the United States is expected to be used by 1986. By the early part of the next century, this new breed of generator will probably produce most of our electricity.

WHAT ARE AMPERES, VOLTS, AND OHMS?

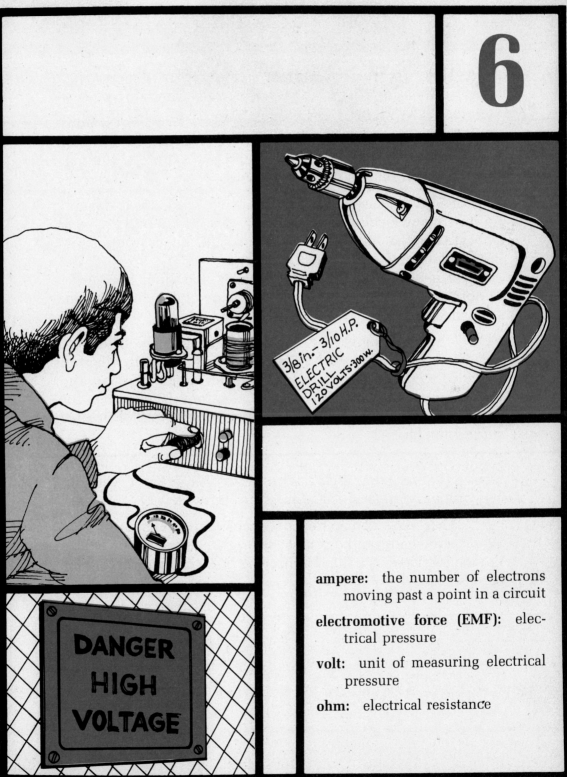

6

ampere: the number of electrons moving past a point in a circuit

electromotive force (EMF): electrical pressure

volt: unit of measuring electrical pressure

ohm: electrical resistance

AIM 6 | What are amperes, volts, and ohms?

How do you measure temperature? In degrees. You measure time in minutes, hours, days, etc. How do you measure length? Weight?

We use different units to measure different things. There are special units to measure electricity too. Three of the most important are *ampere*, *volt*, and *ohm*.

AMPERE [AM peer]   The *size* of an electric current depends on how many electrons pass a point in a circuit every second. The greater the number of electrons, the *larger* the current. Fewer electrons mean a *smaller* current.

The size of an electric current is measured in *amperes* [amps]. We can say that "ampere" is another name for electric current.

VOLT   Nothing moves by itself. A *force* is needed to make something move. Electricity needs a force to move it. Electrons move in a circuit because a force pushes them. The name for the force or pressure that pushes electrons is *electromotive force*. It is often called EMF. *The strength of the EMF is measured in volts.*

OHM [OME]   Ohms measure the *resistance* to the flow of electrons. You know that a wire resists the flow of electrons. *The amount of resistance is measured in ohms.*

There is a connection between amps, volts, and ohms. When one changes, there must be a change in one or both of the others. There is a rule for figuring these changes. It is called *Ohm's Law*.

A.

VOLTS	AMPERES (AMPS)	OHMS
The force that moves electrons in a circuit	The number of electrons that are moving	Resistance—the force that tries to stop or slow the electrons

B.

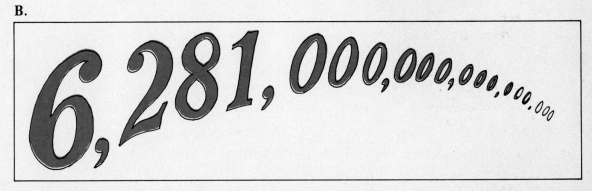

This number of electrons passing a point in a wire every second is *one ampere* of current. Which one is easier to say—one ampere or 6,281,000,000,000,000,000 electrons?

C.

Different electrical devices use different amperes.

- A 100-watt light bulb uses about 1 ampere.

- An electric iron or broiler uses about 10 to 12 amperes.

Fill in the correct answer for each of the following.

1. Another name for *electric current* is _____.

2. Amperes tell us how many _____ move past a point in a circuit every second.

3. EMF stands for _____.

4. Electrical force or pressure is measured in units called _____.

5. Electrical resistance is measured in units called _____.

YOUR OWN WORDS, PLEASE! Use your own words to tell what each of the following is.

1. EMF _____

2. VOLTS _____

3. AMPERES _____

4. OHMS _____

MATCHING Match the two lists. Write the correct letter on the line next to each number.

1. _____ volts

2. _____ amps

3. _____ circuit

4. _____ Ohm's Law

5. _____ ohms

a) electrical resistance

b) path for moving electrons

c) relationship between volts, amps, and ohms

d) electrical pressure

e) number of electrons

Write T on the line next to the number if the sentence is true.
Write F if the sentence is false.

1. _____ EMF stands for a number of electrons.

2. _____ Another name for resistance is *ampere*.

3. _____ Volts describe electrical pressure or force.

4. _____ Different circuits have different amps, volts, and ohms.

5. _____ If volts change, then amps and ohms stay the same.

WORD
SCRAMBLE Unscramble each of the following to form a word or term that
you have read in this Aim.

1. PREAME _____

2. SEPRURES _____

3. MOH _____

4. TOLV _____

5. TRENRUC _____

LET'S
REVIEW Choose one—Choose the correct word or term for each statement.
Write your choice in the space.

1. Electricity that is not moving is called _____ electricity.
static, current

2. Electricity that is moving is called _____ electricity.
static, current

3. Friction produces _____ electricity.
static, current

4. A dry cell produces _____ electricity.
static, current

5. The electricity we use is _____ electricity.
static, current

6. Current electricity is the flow of _____.
atoms, electrons

7. Most current electricity comes from _____.
generators, dry cells

8. The circuit that has only one path to follow is the _____ circuit.
parallel, series

9. The circuit that has more than one path to follow is the _____ circuit.
parallel, series

10. Homes, schools, and factories are wired in _____.
parallel, series

11. "All appliances on or all off" tells us that the circuit is wired in _____.
parallel, series

12. "Any number of appliances on or off" tells us that the circuit is wired in

_____.
parallel, series

13. Change of wire length or thickness _____ change electrical resistance.
does, does not

14. Nichrome is a _____ resistance wire.
high, low

15. A high resistance wire builds _____ heat.
little, much

16. A low resistance wire builds _____ heat.
little, much

17. Copper is a _____ resistance wire.
high, low

18. The size of an electric current is measured in _____.
amperes, volts, ohms

19. Electrical pressure is measured in _____.
amperes, volts, ohms

20. Electrical resistance is measured in _____.
amperes, volts, ohms

44

HOW MUCH FORCE DOES A CIRCUIT NEED?

THIS SIDE UP

45

AIM 7 | How much force does a circuit need?

How hard do you have to push to move a box along the ground? It depends. How many things are in the box? How rough is the ground?

You have to push harder when there are a lot of things in the box. You have to push harder also, when the ground is rough.

- More force is needed to move more things.
- More force is needed when there is greater resistance.

How much force is needed to move electrons in a circuit? It depends on two things:

a) how many electrons must be moved.
b) how much resistance there is.

NUMBER OF ELECTRONS (AMPS)

- More force is needed to move more electrons.
- Less force is needed to move fewer electrons.

RESISTANCE (OHMS)   Resistance slows electrons.

- More force is needed when there is more resistance.
- Less force is needed when there is less resistance.

WHAT DO THE PICTURES SHOW?

Look at the pictures. Then answer the questions. Fill in the blanks. Write A or B in each blank, or choose the correct word.

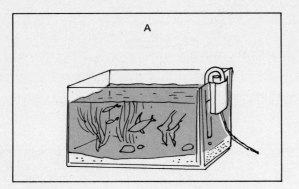

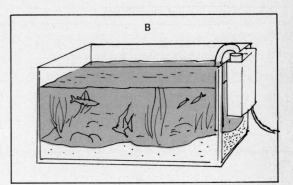

1. Which tank has the larger pump? _____

2. Which tank has the smaller pump? _____

3. Which one pumps more water? _____

4. Which one pumps less water? _____

5. Which pump has more pressure? _____

6. Which pump has less pressure? _____

7. If something were to get stuck in the pipes,

   a) the resistance would _____.

increase, decrease

   b) the water pressure would _____.

increase, decrease

   c) _____ water would flow.

More, Less

8. To fight the resistance, you would need _____ pressure.

more, less

NOW USE THIS THINKING IN WORKING WITH ELECTRICITY!

CHOOSE ONE

Choose the correct word for each statement. Write your choice in the space.

1. _____ force is needed to move more electrons.

More, Less

2. _____ force is needed to move fewer electrons.

More, Less

47

3. Another way of saying this is: more amps need more _____ ; fewer

   amps need fewer_____ .
   ohms, volts

4. With greater resistance _____ electrons move.
   more, fewer

5. With less resistance _____ electrons move.
   more, fewer

6. Another way of saying this is: more ohms means fewer _____ ; fewer
   volts, amps

   ohms means more _____ .
   volts, amps

7. To fight more resistance, you need _____ force.
   more, less

8. Another way of saying this is: more ohms need more _____ .
   volts, amps

WORD SEARCH The words in the list are hidden in the groups of letters. Try to find each word. Draw a line around the word. The spelling may go in any direction: up-and-down, across, or diagonally.

LOAD
VOLT
BATTERY
OHM
HEAT

V	A	T	Y	L
L	O	A	D	E
P	H	L	H	I
A	M	Y	T	R
B	T	R	H	A
A	O	E	A	M
L	A	T	D	O
T	A	T	H	S
L	O	A	L	T
E	T	B	O	S

HOW DO YOU USE A VOLTMETER?

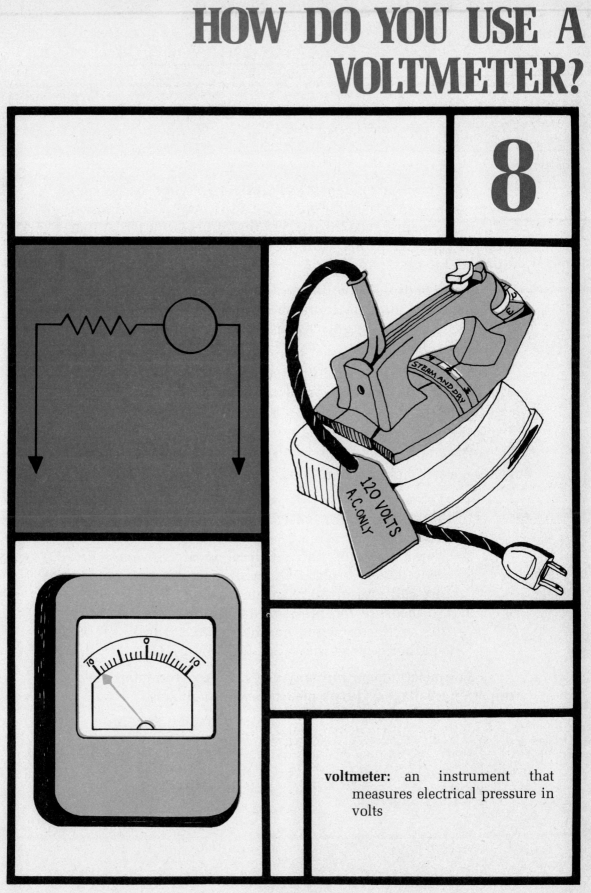

8

voltmeter: an instrument that measures electrical pressure in volts

49

AIM 8 | How do you use a voltmeter?

You have many electrical outlets in your home and school. You also have many electrical appliances. Suppose you bought a new appliance. Its tag said that it needs an outlet that supplies about 115 volts. How would you know if your outlet supplied 115 volts?

You could use a *voltmeter*. A voltmeter measures *electrical pressure*. Electrical pressure or force is measured in volts. For example, the electrical pressure in most homes is about 115 volts.

The symbol for a voltmeter is $-\text{V}-$. A voltmeter can measure the full electrical pressure coming from an outlet or a battery. A voltmeter can also measure the pressure an appliance uses.

Here is how you use a voltmeter. [The pictures on the next page will help explain this.]

1. *To measure the full electrical pressure from an outlet*, just place the voltmeter wires in the socket. Then read the value. [See Figure B.]
2. *To measure the full electrical pressure from a dry cell (battery)*, place the voltmeter's wires on the dry cell's terminals. Read the value. [See Figure C.]
3. *To measure the pressure an appliance uses*, place the voltmeter wires on the *contact points* of the appliance. Read the value. [See Figure D.]

Voltmeters come in many sizes. Some voltmeters measure strong voltages. Others measure weak voltages.

USING A VOLTMETER

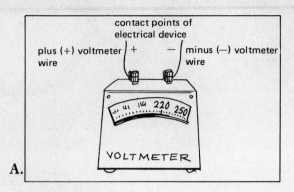

A.

Very important!

- A voltmeter has a plus wire and a minus wire.

- The plus wire goes to the plus end of the electricity.

- The minus wire goes to the minus end of the electricity.

When you connect a voltmeter, you do *not* unhook any wires. You just put the voltmeter wires on the contact points you want to measure. The voltmeter wires just "straddle" the contact points.

B.

Electricians use a voltmeter to measure voltage at a socket.

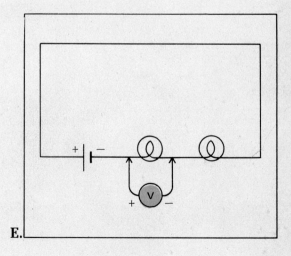

C.

Measuring the voltage of a battery . . .

D.

Measuring the voltage an appliance uses . . . . . →

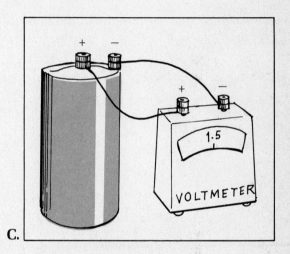

E.

This can be shown in symbol form.

Choose the correct word or term for each statement. Write your choice in the space.

1. Voltage measures _____ .
   electrical resistance, electrical pressure, number of electrons

2. The instrument that measures voltage is called a _____ .
   battery, voltmeter, socket

3. When you connect a voltmeter, you _____ unhook a wire from the circuit.
   do, do not

4. The plus wire of a voltmeter must be connected toward the _____ terminal of a battery.
   plus, minus

5. The minus wire of a voltmeter must be connected toward the _____ end of a socket.
   plus, minus

MATCHING

Match the two lists. Write the correct letter on the line next to each number.

1. _____ voltmeter

2. _____ 115

3. _____ volt

4. _____ plus and minus

5. _____ —Ⓥ—

a) symbol for voltmeter

b) instrument that measures EMF

c) number of volts from most sockets

d) electrical pressure

e) the two ends of an electrical circuit

HOW DO YOU USE AN AMMETER?

9

ammeter: an instrument that measures the number of electrons moving in a circuit

AIM 9 | How do you use an ammeter?

What is an *ammeter* [AM meet er]? An ammeter is an instrument that *measures electric current in amperes*. The symbol for ammeter is Ⓐ.

An ammeter cannot be used the same way as a voltmeter.

An ammeter should *never* be connected to an outlet or to a dry cell. The ammeter would burn out.

Ammeters are used on electrical appliances. An ammeter is *connected right into the circuit*. This is what you have to do. [The pictures on the next page will help explain this.]

1. First, unplug the appliance.
2. Then, unhook a wire of the circuit.
3. Next, connect the ammeter wires to the open ends of the appliance wires.
4. Plug in the appliance.
5. Read the value.

Ammeters come in many sizes. Some ammeters measure small currents. Others measure large currents. It is important to use the right size for the right job.

Electrical instruments damage easily. They should be handled carefully.

AMMETER Only a teacher or an electrician should do this activity.

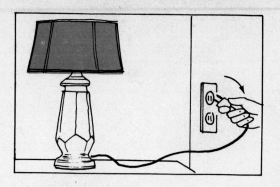

1. Unplug the appliance.

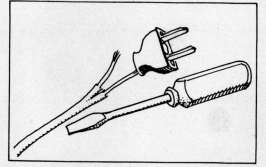

2. Unhook a wire of the circuit.

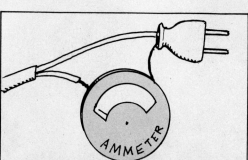

3. Connect the ammeter wires to the open ends of the appliance wires.

4. Plug in the appliance.

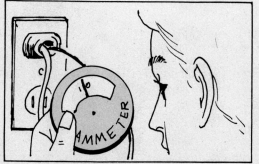

5. Read the value.

HOOKING UP AN AMMETER

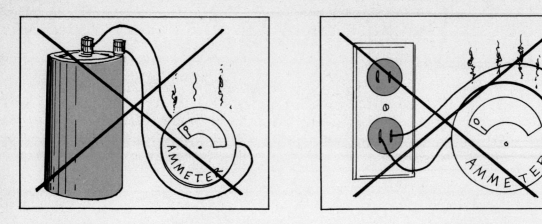

NEVER connect an ammeter to a dry cell or outlet.

COMPLETING SENTENCES Complete the sentences with the choices below. One of these may be used twice.

-Ⓥ-
amperes
voltmeter

ammeter
-Ⓐ-

electric current
volts

1. Electrical pressure is measured in units called _____.

2. A _____ measures electrical pressure.

3. The number of electrons in a circuit is measured in units called _____.
   (one word)

4. An _____ measures the number of electrons moving across a point in a circuit.

5. Amperes are a measure of _____.

6. The symbol for a voltmeter is _____.

7. The symbol for an ammeter is _____.

8. The instrument you should never connect to a battery or outlet is the

_____.

WORKING WITH CIRCUITS

Study the symbol drawings below.
Then answer the questions below the drawings.

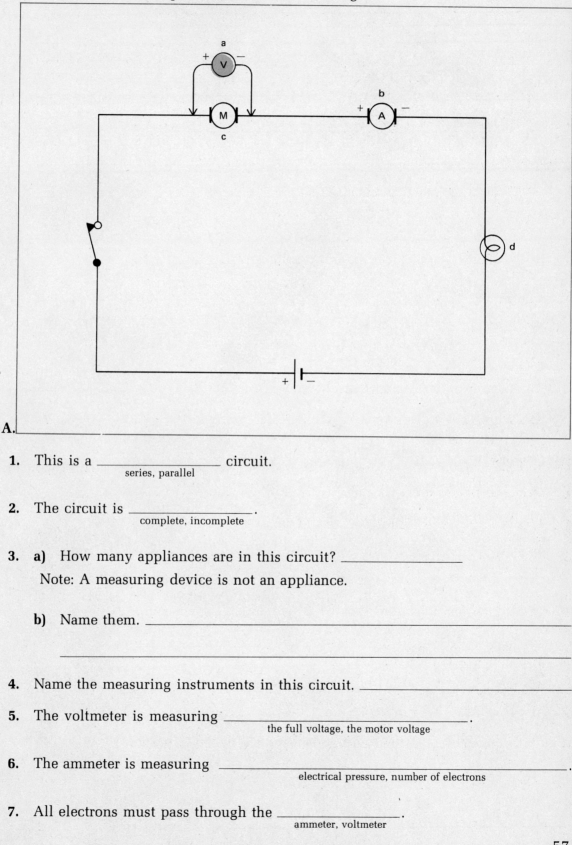

A.

1. This is a _____ circuit.
   _{series, parallel}

2. The circuit is _____.
   _{complete, incomplete}

3. a) How many appliances are in this circuit? _____
   Note: A measuring device is not an appliance.

   b) Name them. _____

   _____

4. Name the measuring instruments in this circuit. _____

5. The voltmeter is measuring _____.
   _{the full voltage, the motor voltage}

6. The ammeter is measuring _____.
   _{electrical pressure, number of electrons}

7. All electrons must pass through the _____.
   _{ammeter, voltmeter}

57

B.

1. This is a _____ circuit.
   series, parallel

2. **a)** How many appliances are in this circuit? _____

   Note: A measuring device is not an appliance.

   b) Name them. **a)** _____ **b)** _____

   c) _____ **d)** _____

3. The measuring instruments are shown in color and labeled I, II, III, IV, V, and VI.

   a) Which ones are voltmeters? _____

   b) Which ones are ammeters? _____

4. **a)** Which ones measure electric *current?* _____

   b) Which ones measure electric *pressure?* _____

5. Is instrument III measuring the current from appliance b or c? *(Remember, electricity flows from minus to plus.)* _____

6. **a)** Which instruments will show no readings? _____

   b) Why? _____

REACHING OUT   A *voltmeter* measures electrical *pressure;* an *ammeter* measures electrical *current.*

What do you think we call the instrument that measures electrical *resistance?*

_____

_____

WHAT IS A MAGNETIC SUBSTANCE?

magnet: a metal that can attract certain other metals

lodestone: a rock that is a magnet

magnetite: another name for lodestone

alloy: two or more metals melted together

alnico:
Permalloy: } two alloys that can be made into strong magnets

AIM 10 | What is a magnetic substance?

How do you use magnets? To hold notes on a refrigerator door? To pick up pins or tacks? Did you ever wonder why a magnet works the way it does? A penny won't stick to a refrigerator door. It won't pick up pins or tacks. A magnet will!

What *is* a magnet? Why does it act the way it does? Why don't other things act like magnets?

Only certain materials can become magnets. A material that can become a magnet is called a *magnetic substance*. A magnetic substance can also be *picked up by a magnet*.

There are only three good magnetic substances. They are the metals *iron*, *nickel*, and *cobalt*. Iron is the most magnetic.

One kind of magnet is found in nature. The rock *magnetite* [MAG nuh tite] is a *natural magnet*. It has bits of iron in it. Magnetite is also called *lodestone*. Most magnets are not natural. They are made by people. Such magnets are called *artificial magnets*.

Most artificial magnets are made of *alloys* [AL oiz]. An alloy is a mixture of metals melted together. Steel is an important alloy. Most magnets are made of steel. Two other alloys are used to make extra-strong magnets. These alloys are *alnico* [AL nick oe] and *Permalloy* [PUR muh loy]. Both alloys contain one or more of the three magnetic substances.

Magnets are made in many sizes, shapes, and strengths. Magnets have many uses.

MAGNETS

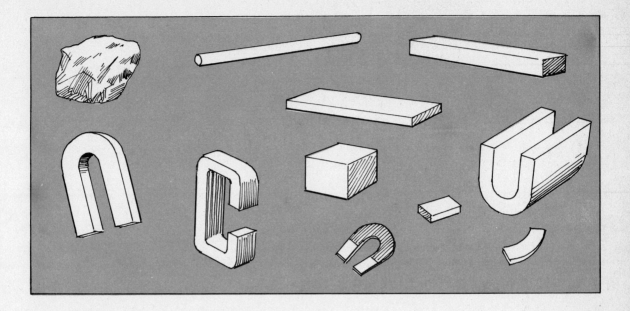

Magnets come in many sizes and shapes.

Magnetic iron (lodestone) was discovered about 2,000 years ago in a part of Asia called *Magnesia*.

The terms *magnet* and *magnetism* come from this place.

COMPLETING SENTENCES Complete the sentences with the choices below. One of these may be used twice.

---

iron	magnetite	Permalloy
alloy	picked up	nickel
artificial	people	natural
magnet	cobalt	lodestone
alnico		

1. A magnetic substance is a substance that can be _____ by a magnet.

2. A magnetic substance can also be made into a _____.

3. The three good magnetic substances are: _____, _____, and _____.

4. The metal found in most magnets is _____.

5. Magnets that are found in nature are called _____ magnets.

61

6. The name of a natural magnet is _____. It is also called

_____.

7. The opposite of natural is _____.

8. Most magnets are made by _____.

9. A mixture of metals melted together is called an _____.

10. Very powerful magnets are made of the alloys _____ and _____

_____.

TESTING FOR MAGNETIC SUBSTANCES

Touch each substance listed below with a magnet. See if it is magnetic or nonmagnetic. Put a check [√] in the proper box.

The last two lines have been left blank. Select two materials not on the list. Test them and write the results on lines 9 and 10.

		Magnetic	Nonmagnetic
1.	glass		
2.	iron nail		
3.	paper		
4.	plastic		
5.	nickel (not a coin)		
6.	copper		
7.	cobalt		
8.	steel (not stainless)		
9.			
10.			

TRUE OR FALSE

Write T on the line next to the number if the sentence is true. Write F if the sentence is false.

1. _____ A magnet is never found in nature.

2. _____ All magnets are found in nature.

3. _____ Lodestone is a natural magnet.

4. _____ Iron is a magnetic substance.

5. _____ Iron is an alloy.

6. _____ Steel is an alloy.

7. _____ Most magnets are made of steel.

8. _____ The strongest magnets are made of steel.

9. _____ Copper is a magnetic substance.

10. _____ Most substances are magnetic.

MATCHING

Match the two lists. Write the correct letter on the line next to each number.

1. _____ iron, nickel, and cobalt   a) not found in nature

2. _____ natural magnet   b) good magnetic substances

3. _____ steel   c) found in nature

4. _____ artificial   d) alloy

5. _____ natural   e) lodestone

WORD SCRAMBLE Unscramble each of the following to form a word or term that you have read in this Aim.

1. BLATCO _____

2. GETMAN _____

3. LETNODEOS _____

4. YOLAL _____

5. CAINOL _____

REACHING OUT You can buy strips of "magnetic" rubber and plastic.

1. Is plastic rubber or plastic *really* magnetic? _____

2. How is plastic and rubber made to stick like a magnet? _____

_____

HOW DO MAGNETS BEHAVE?

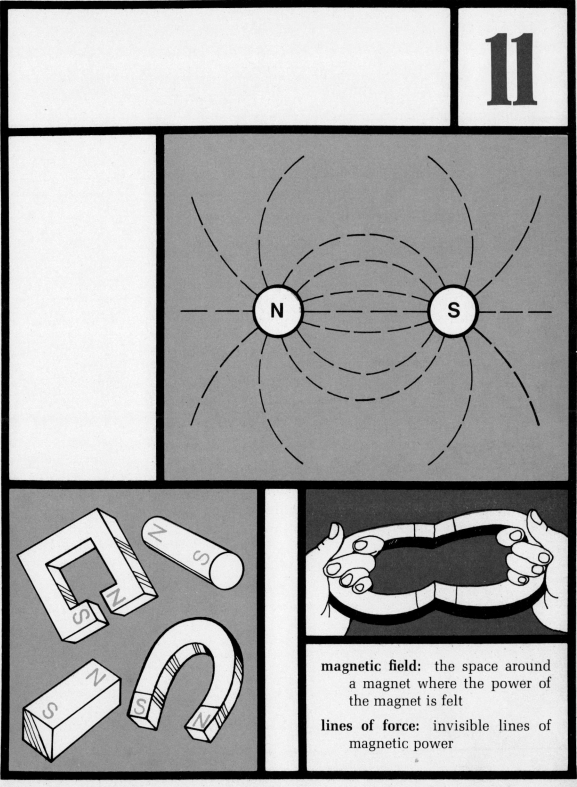

11

magnetic field: the space around a magnet where the power of the magnet is felt

lines of force: invisible lines of magnetic power

AIM 11 | How do magnets behave?

What are the different shapes magnets come in? Have you seen horseshoe-shaped magnets? bar-shaped magnets? No matter what shape a magnet comes in it has two ends—no more and no less than two. *Every magnet has two ends.*

The ends of a magnet are called *poles*. One pole is the *north pole*. The other is the *south pole*. A magnet gives off energy. You cannot see the energy. It is strongest at the poles. The energy is weakest in the middle.

If you hold two magnets together, what happens? The answer depends on the poles! If you hold two north poles together, they push apart. The same will happen with two south poles—they push apart. Two north poles are alike—they are *like* poles. Two south poles are also like poles. *Like poles repel.*

What happens if you hold a north and south pole together? They pull together. A north pole and a south pole are not alike—they are *unlike* poles. *Unlike poles attract.*

Magnetic energy spreads out in all directions. The energy is made up of many *lines of force.* You cannot see them. All the lines of force make up what is called a *magnetic field.*

A magnet's power is felt within its magnetic field. The field is strongest close to the magnet. The magnetic field grows weaker the farther you get from the magnet.

WHAT DO THE PICTURES SHOW?

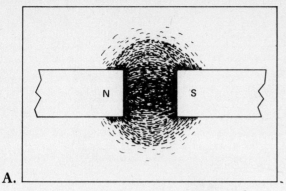

A. Magnetic field between *unlike* poles.

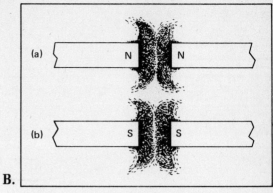

B. Magnetic field between *like* poles.

Look at each picture. Then answer the questions.

C.

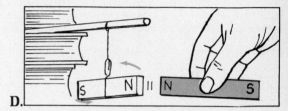

D.

1. **a)** The hand in Figure C is holding the south pole close to the

   _____ pole of the
   north, south
   hanging magnet.

   b) They are _____ poles.
   like, unlike

   c) The poles _____.
   attract, repel

3. CONCLUSION: *Like* poles _____.
   attract, repel

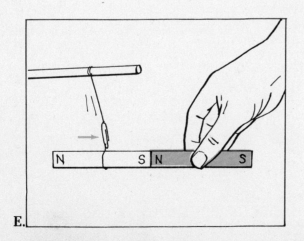

E.

2. **a)** The hand in Figure D is holding the north pole close to the

   _____ pole of the
   north, south
   hanging magnet.

   b) They are _____ poles.
   like, unlike

   c) The poles _____.
   attract, repel

4. **a)** The hand in Figure **E** is holding the north pole close to the

   _____ pole of the
   north, south
   hanging magnet.

   b) They are _____ poles.
   like, unlike

   c) The poles _____.
   attract, repel

5. CONCLUSION: *Unlike* poles

   _____.
   attract, repel

HOW TO MAKE A "MAP" OF A MAGNETIC FIELD

What You Need

bar magnet
thin sheet of paper
iron filings

How To Do The Experiment

1. Place the magnet on a table.
2. Cover the magnet with the paper.
3. Gently sprinkle the iron filings on the paper.

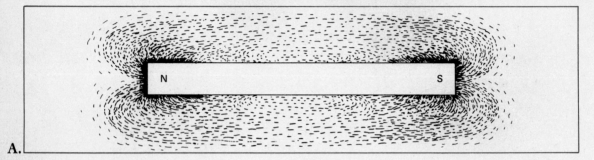

A.

What You Learned

Your "map" should look something like this. Study the "map." Then answer these questions.

1. Most of the iron filings are at _____.
   the poles, the middle

2. There are fewer iron filings at _____.
   the poles, the middle

3. A magnet is strongest at _____.
   the poles, the middle

4. A magnet is weakest at _____.
   the poles, the middle

5. Most iron filings are _____ the magnet.
   close to, far from

6. As you move away from the magnet, there are _____ iron filings.
   more, fewer

7. A magnetic field is strongest _____ a magnet.
   close to, far from

8. As you move away from a magnet, the magnetic field becomes _____.
   stronger, weaker

WORKING WITH MAGNETIC FIELDS

The diagram below shows a bar magnet and its magnetic field. A, B, C, and D are pieces of iron.

Study the diagram. Then answer the questions.

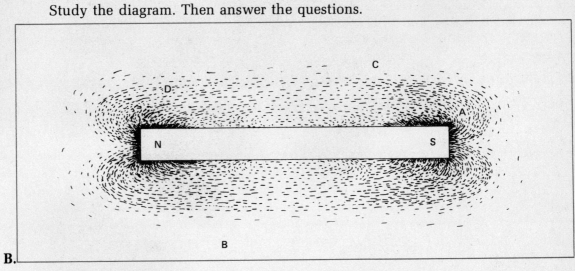

1. Which pieces of iron are *outside* the magnetic field? _____

2. Which pieces of iron are *inside* the magnetic field? _____

3. Look at the pieces that are inside the magnetic field.

   a) Which one does the magnet attract *more*? _____

   b) Which one does the magnet attract *less*? _____

EXPERIMENT WITH MAGNETISM

Aim: To find out which substances let magnetic energy pass through them and which substances do not.

What You Need

magnet
stand with clamp
thin string
steel paper clip
thin pieces of materials listed on the next page

How To Do The Experiment Set up the materials as shown on page 69.

Then, one at a time, hold the materials listed below between the clip and the magnet. Notice what happens. Does the paper clip drop?

Fill in the chart.

Material	Does the paper clip drop? [Yes or No]
1. paper	
2. cloth	
3. iron	
4. cobalt	
5. glass	
6. plastic	
7. nickel	

What You Learned

1. Which materials did *not* make the paper clip drop? _____

_____

2. **a)** Paper, cloth, glass, and plastic are _____ substances.
   <u>magnetic, non-magnetic</u>

   b) Magnetic energy _____ go through these substances.
   <u>does, does not</u>

3. Magnetic energy _____ pass through non-magnetic substances.
   <u>does, does not</u>

4. Which materials *did* make the paper clip drop? _____

5. **a)** Iron, nickel, and cobalt are _____ substances.
   <u>magnetic, non-magnetic</u>

   b) Magnetic energy _____ go through these substances.
   <u>does, does not</u>

6. Magnetic energy _____ go through magnetic substances.
   <u>does, does not</u>

Conclusion

7. _____ substances do *not* affect a magnetic field.
   <u>Magnetic, Non-magnetic</u>

8. _____ substances *do* affect a magnetic field.
   <u>Magnetic, Non-magnetic</u>

COMPLETING SENTENCES Complete the sentences with the choices below. Three of these may be used twice.

unlike poles   south pole
like poles   poles
repel   attract
magnetic field   north pole

1. The ends of a magnet are called _____.
   (one word)

2. One end of a magnet is called the _____; the other end is called the

   _____.

3. A south pole and south pole, or a north pole and north pole are called _____

   _____.

4. A north pole and south pole are called _____.

5. Like poles _____.

6. Unlike poles _____.

7. Two north poles or two south poles will _____.

8. A north pole and a south pole will _____.

9. The space around a magnet where the power of a magnet is felt is called its

   _____.

10. A magnet is strongest at the _____.

MATCHING Match the two lists. Write the correct letter on the line next to each number.

1. _____ like poles   a) make up magnetic field

2. _____ unlike poles   b) magnetic substances

3. _____ lines of force   c) repel

4. _____ center of a magnet   d) attract

5. _____ iron, nickel, cobalt e) weakest part

TRUE OR FALSE

Write T on the line next to the number if the sentence is true. Write F if the sentence is false.

1. _____ A north pole and a north pole are like poles.

2. _____ Two north poles are the only like poles.

3. _____ Like poles attract.

4. _____ A north pole and a south pole are unlike poles.

5. _____ Unlike poles repel.

6. _____ Lines of force are invisible.

7. _____ A magnet is strongest at the middle.

8. _____ Glass and paper let magnetic energy pass through them.

9. _____ Glass and paper are magnetic substances.

10. _____ Iron lets magnetic energy pass through it.

11. _____ Iron is a magnetic substance.

THROW ONE OUT

In each of the following set of terms, one of the terms does *not* belong. Circle that term.

1. magnetic substance   glass   iron
2. natural magnet   cobalt   lodestone
3. aluminum   iron   cobalt
4. alloy   nickel   alnico
5. artificial   factory-made   nature-made

WHAT CHANGES TAKE PLACE WHEN A SUBSTANCE BECOMES A MAGNET?

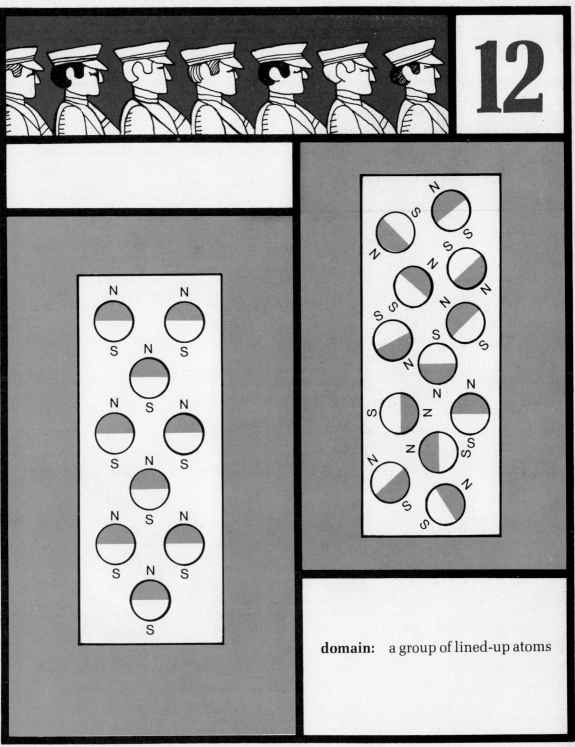

12

domain: a group of lined-up atoms

AIM 12 | What changes take place when a substance becomes a magnet?

Soldiers are standing around in no set order. The captain shouts, "ATTENTION!" The soldiers line up in neat rows. They are ready to act together.

Something like that happens when a substance is magnetized. An atom is the smallest part of a substance. Every atom has a north pole and a south pole. When the substance is *not* a magnet, the atoms face in many directions. They are *not* lined up. The magnetic forces of the different atoms work against one another. Their magnetic power is not felt.

When a substance becomes a magnet, many atoms group together. Each group acts like a magnet. All the north poles face one way. All the south poles face the opposite way. The magnetic power is felt because the atoms *work together*. The whole piece becomes a magnet.

A group of lined-up atoms is called a *domain* [doe MAIN]. A magnet has millions of domains. If a magnet breaks, each piece still has domains. Each piece is a magnet. The smallest piece of a magnet is just one domain.

Only atoms of iron, nickel, and cobalt can form domains. They are the only magnetic substances. All magnetic alloys contain iron, nickel or cobalt.

WHAT DO THE PICTURES SHOW?

Look at each picture. Then answer the questions.

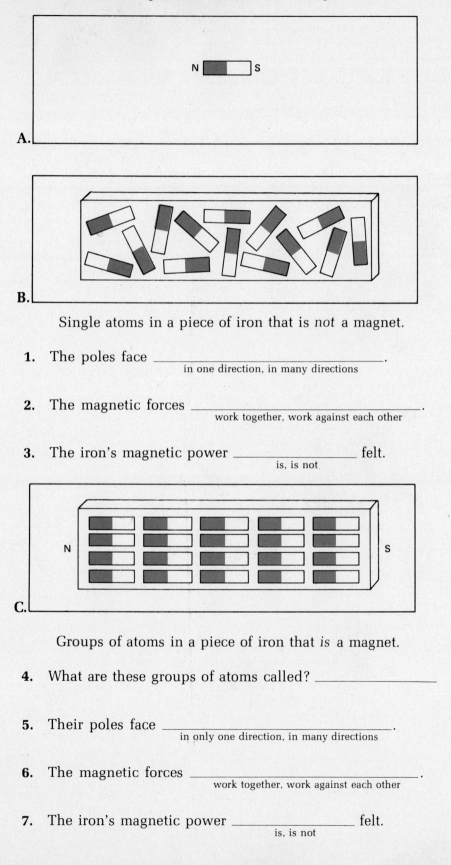

Single atoms in a piece of iron that is *not* a magnet.

1. The poles face _____.
in one direction, in many directions

2. The magnetic forces _____.
work together, work against each other

3. The iron's magnetic power _____ felt.
is, is not

Groups of atoms in a piece of iron that *is* a magnet.

4. What are these groups of atoms called? _____

5. Their poles face _____.
in only one direction, in many directions

6. The magnetic forces _____.
work together, work against each other

7. The iron's magnetic power _____ felt.
is, is not

D.

This is a bar magnet.

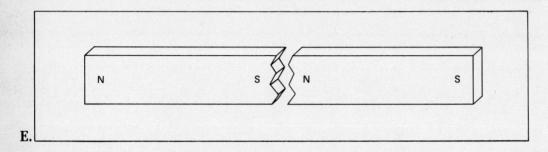

E.

This is the same bar magnet broken in half.

8. Does breaking a magnet destroy the magnet? _____

9. How would *four* pieces look? Draw the picture in the box below. Label the poles.

F.

10. How many magnets do you have now? _____

11. What is the smallest part of any magnet? _____

COMPLETING SENTENCES

Complete the sentences with the choices below.

work together   domains   one domain
magnet   in all directions   ten
one direction

1. Every atom of a magnetic substance is like a tiny _____.

2. The atoms of matter that is not a magnet face _____.

3. The atoms of a magnet form groups called _____.

4. The poles of domains line up in _____.

5. The magnetic powers of domains _____.

6. The smallest part of a magnet is _____.

7. If you break a magnet into ten pieces, you end up with _____ magnets.

TRUE OR FALSE

Write T on the line next to the number if the sentence is true. Write F if the sentence is false.

1. _____ Wood is a magnetic substance.

2. _____ Iron is a magnetic substance.

3. _____ Every piece of iron has domains.

4. _____ Magnetized iron has domains.

5. _____ Only magnets have domains.

6. _____ Domains work against each other.

7. _____ A domain is larger than an atom.

8. _____ A magnet has only two poles.

9. _____ A magnet can have two north poles.

10. _____ You can destroy a magnet by breaking it.

Choose the correct word or term for each statement. Write your choice in the space.

1. Atoms normally _____ lined up.
   _{are, are not}

2. You have a piece of iron that is not a magnet. The atoms _____
   lined up.   _{are, are not}

3. The atoms of iron _____ be made to line up.
   _{can, cannot}

4. A substance with lined-up atoms is called _____.
   _{an alloy, a magnet}

5. A group of lined-up atoms is called a _____.
   _{magnetic field, domain}

6. Substances like wood, glass, and plastic _____ form domains.
   _{do, do not}

7. Iron, nickel, and cobalt _____ form domains.
   _{do, do not}

WORD SCRAMBLE   Unscramble each of the following to form a word or term that you have read in this Aim.

1. MOANID   _____

2. LICKEN   _____

3. MOAT   _____

4. POURG   _____

5. RONI   _____

WHAT ARE TEMPORARY AND PERMANENT MAGNETS?

13

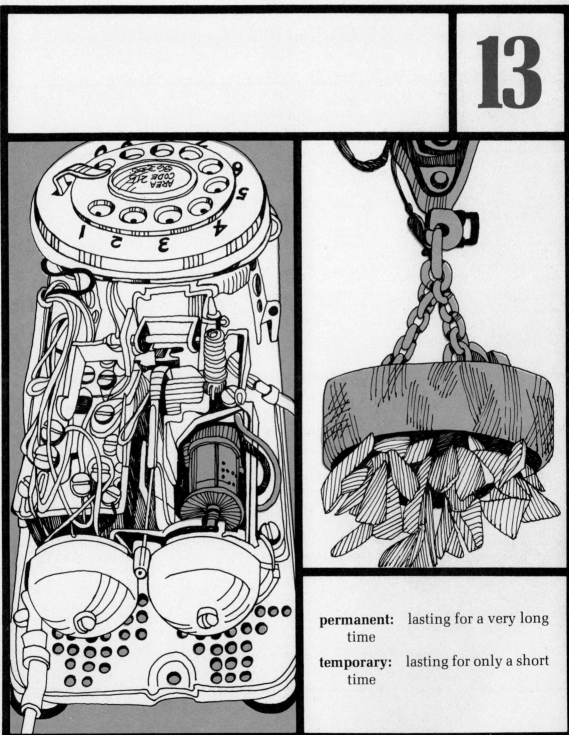

permanent: lasting for a very long time

temporary: lasting for only a short time

AIM 13 | What are temporary and permanent magnets?

You probably know the word *temporary* [TEM puh reh ree]. Maybe you know someone who had a temporary job. It lasted for a short time—a week, a month, a summer. The opposite of temporary is *permanent* [PUR muh nent]. A permanent job lasts for a very long time—years and years.

Something that lasts a short time is temporary. Something that lasts a *very* long time is permanent. Things that are permanent seem to last forever.

Some magnets are temporary magnets. Others are permanent magnets.

TEMPORARY MAGNETS

Temporary magnets keep their magnetism for only a short time. Then they lose the magnetism.

Most temporary magnets are made of soft iron. Soft iron becomes a magnet very easily. But soft iron loses its magnetism easily.

PERMANENT MAGNETS

Permanent magnets keep their magnetism. They can be used over and over again. The magnets you use in class are permanent magnets. So are the magnets in your home.

Most permanent magnets are made of steel. Steel does not become a magnet as easily as iron does. But once steel becomes a magnet, it keeps its magnetism.

There are extra-strong permanent magnets. They are made of alnico and Permalloy.

TEMPORARY AND PERMANENT MAGNETS

A.

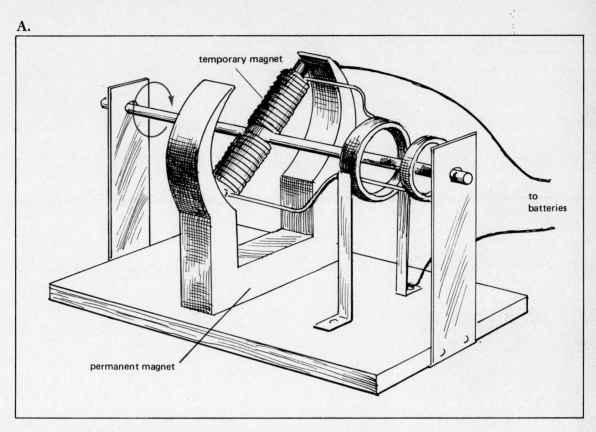

A motor has temporary *and* permanent magnets.

B.   **C.**

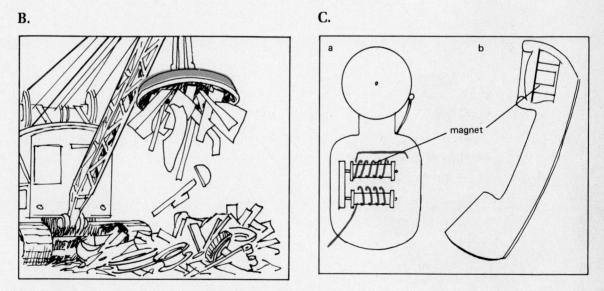

Some temporary magnets are *electromagnets*.

They have many uses. For example, large electromagnets are used to lift heavy pieces of iron. Electromagnets are also needed in telephones and bells.

COMPLETING SENTENCES

Complete the sentences with the choices below.

permanent
temporary
magnetism
loses

Permalloy
steel
soft iron
alnico

alloy
lasting a short time
easily
lasting a long time

1. Temporary means _____.

2. Permanent means _____.

3. A magnet is permanent or temporary depending how long it keeps its

   _____.

4. Magnets that keep their magnetism for a short time are _____ magnets.

5. Magnets that keep their magnetism for a long time are _____.

6. Temporary magnets are made of _____.

7. Soft iron becomes a magnet _____. Soft iron also

   _____ its magnetism easily.

8. Most permanent magnets are made of _____.

9. Steel is an _____ of iron.

10. Extra strong permanent magnets are made of the alloys _____

    and _____.

MATCHING

Match the two lists. Write the correct letter on the line next to each number.

1. _____ permanent

2. _____ temporary

3. _____ soft iron

4. _____ steel

5. _____ alnico and Permalloy

a) used for most permanent magnets

b) become extra strong permanent magnets

c) lasting a short time

d) lasting a long time

e) used to make temporary magnets

TRUE OR FALSE

Write T on the line next to the number if the sentence is true. Write F if the sentence is false.

1. _____ All magnets have the same power.

2. _____ All magnets keep their magnetism.

3. _____ Soft iron becomes a magnet easily.

4. _____ Soft iron loses its magnetism easily.

5. _____ Steel becomes a magnet easily.

6. _____ Steel loses its magnetism easily.

7. _____ Soft iron magnets are permanent magnets.

8. _____ Steel magnets are permanent magnets.

9. _____ Alnico magnets are temporary magnets.

10. _____ Every alloy has iron in it.

THROW ONE OUT

In each of the following sets of terms, one of the terms does not belong. Circle that term.

1. temporary magnet   steel   soft iron

2. steel   soft iron   permanent magnet

3. iron   steel   alloy

4. magnetic   paper   iron

5. non-magnetic   paper   nickel

WORD SCRAMBLE

Unscramble each of the following to form a word or term that you have read in this Aim.

1. MANTENREP _____

2. MERATYPOR _____

3. LEMPRYLOA _____

4. LESET _____

5. SROGNT _____

REACHING OUT

Does anything last *forever*? What about a giant mountain?

_____

_____

_____

_____

_____

_____

HOW CAN YOU MAKE A MAGNET?

contact: to touch

AIM 14 | How can you make a magnet?

There are several ways to make magnets. But you always have to start out with a magnetic substance. Two ways of making magnets are by *contact* and by *stroking*.

MAGNETIZING BY CONTACT

The word *contact* means "touch." When a magnet touches a magnetic substance, the substance also becomes a magnet. The magnetic energy in the magnet makes the atoms in the substance line up. The atoms line up into domains. Contact magnetism can be passed on from one magnetic substance to another.

For example, look at Figure A on the facing page. The magnet has picked up tacks. Some tacks are not touching the magnet. They are only touching *other* tacks. The magnetism has been passed from one tack to the next one. Each tack has become a magnet by *contact*.

Magnets that are made by contact are very weak. The magnetism does not last long. Contact magnets are *temporary* magnets.

MAGNETIZING BY STROKING

You can make a piece of steel into a magnet by stroking the steel with a permanent magnet. But you have to stroke the steel in a special way:

1. Stroke the steel with just *one pole* of the magnet.
2. Stroke the steel in just *one direction*.

Magnets that are made by stroking are permanent magnets. But they are usually weak magnets.

WHAT DO THE PICTURES SHOW?

Look at each picture. Then answer the questions.

A.

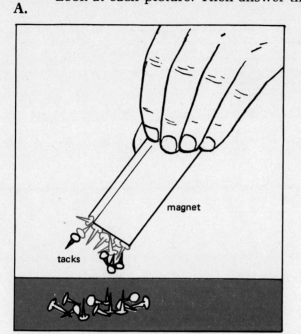

Only the tacks in color are touching the magnet. . . . They have become magnets by *contact.*

See how the magnetism is passed on from tack to tack.

Each tack becomes a magnet by contact.

1. Magnets made by contact are _____ magnets.
<u>temporary, permanent</u>

B.

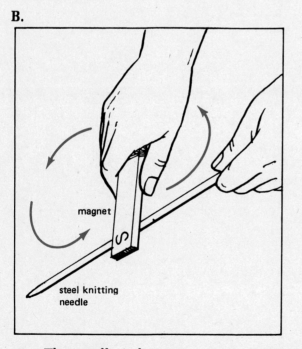

2. The needle is becoming a magnet by _____.
<u>contact, stroking</u>

3. The stroking is done with _____ _____ of a permanent magnet.
<u>only one pole, both poles</u>

4. The stroking is done _____ _____.
<u>back and forth, in only one direction</u>

5. The needle is becoming a _____ magnet.
<u>permanent, temporary</u>

6. The needle will be a _____ magnet.
<u>strong, weak</u>

7. The needle is made of _____.
<u>steel, soft iron</u>

87

COMPLETING SENTENCES

Complete the sentences with the choices below. Two of these may be used twice.

permanent
magnet

temporary
one pole

touch
in one direction only

1. To "contact" means to _____.

2. A magnetic substance becomes a magnet if it is touching a _____.

3. Magnets made by contact are _____ magnets.

4. Magnets made by stroking are _____ magnets.

5. Steel can become only a _____ magnet.

6. Soft iron can become only a _____ magnet.

7. To make a magnet by stroking, you stroke steel _____,

    with only _____ of a permanent magnet.

TRUE FALSE

Write T on the line next to the number if the sentence is true. Write F if the sentence is false.

1. _____ Every metal can become a magnet.

2. _____ Soft iron can become a permanent magnet.

3. _____ When you are standing, your feet are in contact with the ground.

4. _____ Magnets made by contact are temporary magnets.

5. _____ Steel can become a permanent magnet by stroking.

6. _____ Back and forth stroking makes steel a magnet.

7. _____ An alloy has one metal.

8. _____ Alnico magnets are temporary magnets.

9. _____ We need magnetism to make a magnet. (Think about this one.)

TESTING A MAGNET

Make your own magnet by stroking.
See how extra strokings change its strength.

What You Need permanent magnet
steel knitting needle
small steel straight pins

How To Do the Experiment

1. Place the tip of the needle into the pins. Then lift the needle. How many pins does it lift?

   Write your answer on the chart.

2. Stroke the needle twenty times in one direction with the magnet. How many pins does the needle lift?

   Write the number on the chart.

3. Do the same thing for 40, 60, 80, and 100 strokes. Write down the number of pins lifted.

Number of Strokes	Number of Pins Lifted
0	
20	
40	
60	
80	
100	

4. The more you stroke the needle, the _____ pins it picks up.
   <u>more, fewer</u>

5. The more you stroke the needle, the _____ a magnet it becomes.
   <u>stronger, weaker</u>

6. There _____ a limit to how strong a magnet the needle can become.
   <u>is, is not</u>
   (Take a guess.)

HOW CAN YOU MAKE A MAGNET BY INDUCTION?

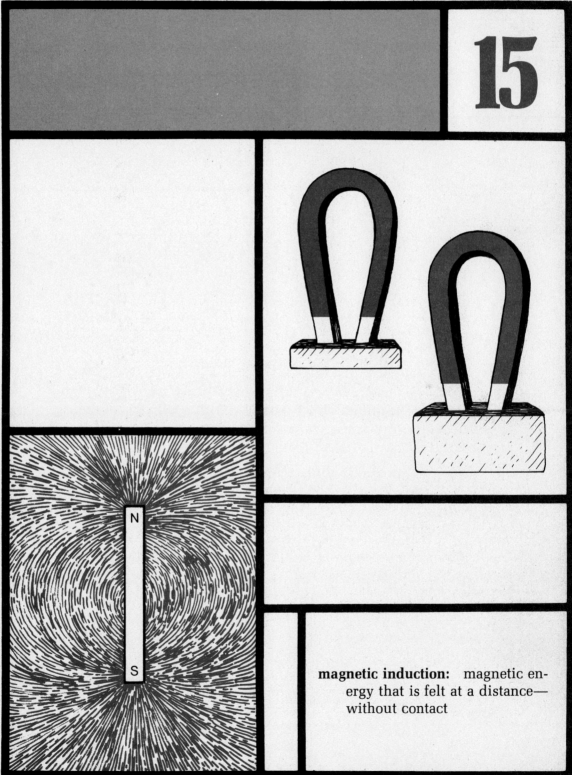

magnetic induction: magnetic energy that is felt at a distance—without contact

AIM 15 | How can you make a magnet by induction?

If you touch a fire, you get burned. But you don't have to actually *touch* a flame to get burned. You can get burned just by being *near* a flame—Heat energy spreads out. It can be felt at a *distance* from the flame.

Magnetic energy also spreads out. The energy can be felt at a *distance* from a magnet. Because of this, a magnetic substance can become a magnet just by being *near* a magnet.

This way of making a magnet is called *induction* [in DUCK shun]. Magnetic induction works best in a strong magnetic field. Induction works less well in a weak magnetic field. There can be no induction outside the magnetic field.

Both temporary and permanent magnets can be made by induction. Which kind you get depends on two things:

1. the kind of metal
2. the strength of the magnetic field.

Iron can become a temporary magnet only. Iron can be magnetized by induction very easily. Even a weak magnetic field will work. But iron does not keep its magnetism. It loses it when the magnetic field is removed.

Steel can become a permanent magnet only. Steel cannot be magnetized easily by induction. A very strong magnetic field is needed. But steel keeps its magnetism once it *does* become a magnet.

The strong magnetic fields needed to make permanent magnets come from electricity.

WHAT DOES THE PICTURE SHOW?

This diagram shows a magnet, its magnetic field, and four pieces of iron.

Study the diagram. Then answer the questions.

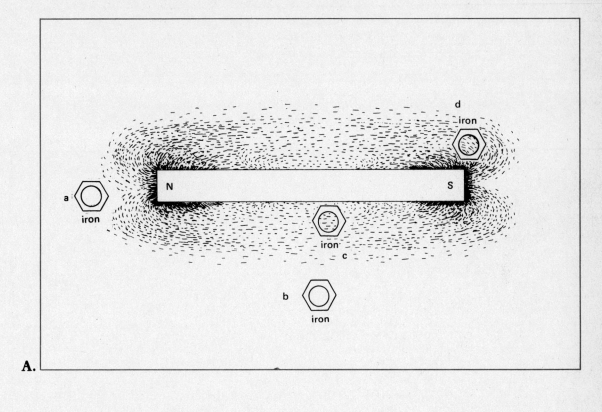

A.

1. **a)** Which iron pieces are *inside* the magnetic field? _____

    b) Which iron pieces are *outside* the magnetic field? _____

2. **a)** Which iron pieces *have* become magnets? _____

    b) Which iron pieces have *not* become magnets? _____

3. Look at the pieces that *have* become magnets.

    a) Which one is *stronger*? _____

    b) Which one is *weaker*? _____

4. The iron pieces that have become magnets, have become magnets by

    _____ .
    contact, induction, stroking

5. Magnetic induction takes place _____ a magnetic field.
    inside, outside

STUDYING MAGNETIC INDUCTION

What You Need magnet
large iron nail
small steel tacks

How To Do the Experiment

A.

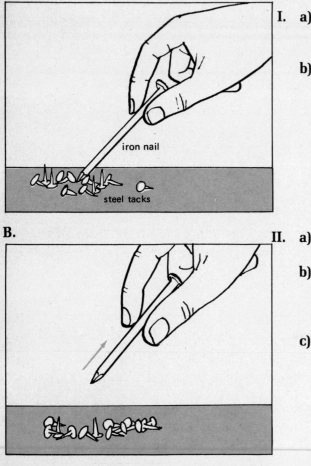

iron nail

steel tacks

B.

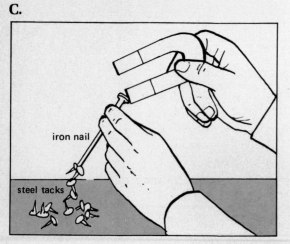

C.

iron nail

steel tacks

I. a) Hold the end of the nail in the pile of tacks (Figure **A**).

  b) Lift the nail (Figure **B**).

  1. The nail _____ lift
  _{does, does not}
  any tacks.

  2. This shows that the nail

  _____ a magnet.
  _{is, is not}

II. a) Place the nail in the tacks again.

  b) With your other hand, hold the magnet *close to* the head of the nail. (Careful, don't let them touch.)

  c) Lift the nail and magnet together (Figure **C**). (Careful, keep the distance between the nail and the magnet.)

  3. The nail _____ lift
  _{does, does not}
  any tacks.

  4. The nail _____ be-
  _{has, has not}
  come a magnet.

  5. The magnet and nail

  _____ touching.
  _{are, are not}

  6. The nail _____ in
  _{is, is not}
  the magnetic field of the magnet.

  7. By what method has the nail become a magnet? _____

94

D.

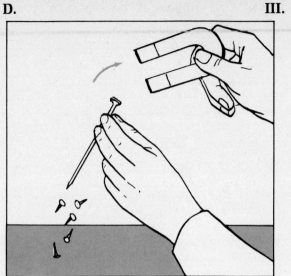

III. Pull the magnet away [Figure **D**].

8. The tacks _____ do, do not drop.

9. The nail _____ is still, is no longer in the magnetic field of the magnet.

10. The nail has _____ kept, lost its magnetism.

11. Iron can become only a _____ _____ magnet. permanent, temporary

COMPLETING SENTENCES Complete the sentences with the choices below. Two of these may be used twice.

induction	contact	temporary
does not	weak	electricity
very strong	permanent	stroking
very easily		

1. Two ways to make a magnet by touching are by _____ and by _____.

2. Magnetism at a distance is called _____.

3. Both _____ and _____ magnets are made by induction.

4. Iron can become only a _____ magnet.

5. Iron becomes a magnet _____.

6. Even a _____ magnetic field can make iron a magnet by induction.

7. Induction makes steel into a _____ magnet.

8. Steel _____ become a magnet by induction easily.

9. A _____ magnetic field is needed to make steel a permanent magnet by induction.

10. Very strong magnetic fields come from _____.

TRUE OR FALSE

Write T on the line next to the number if the sentence is true. Write F if the sentence is false.

1. _____ "Stroking" is magnetism at a distance.

2. _____ "Contact" magnetism is magnetism at a distance.

3. _____ "Induction" is magnetism at a distance.

4. _____ Induction works only inside a magnetic field.

5. _____ Iron can become a magnet by induction.

6. _____ Iron becomes a permanent magnet.

7. _____ Iron becomes a magnet easily.

8. _____ Steel can become a magnet by induction.

9. _____ Steel becomes a magnet easily by induction.

10. _____ Steel becomes a temporary magnet.

WORD SEARCH

The words in this list are hidden in the groups of letters. Try to find each word. Draw a line around the word. The spelling may go in any direction: up-and-down, across, or diagonally.

MAGNET
IRON
ALLOY
ALNICO
NICKEL
COBALT
LODESTONE
DOMAIN

E	I	N	I	A	M	O	D
N	R	R	E	T	S	T	O
O	O	N	O	D	E	K	C
T	P	G	O	N	C	D	I
S	E	L	G	I	K	L	N
E	Y	A	Y	C	N	E	L
D	M	O	O	K	L	G	A
O	A	B	L	E	O	L	N
L	P	N	I	L	Y	I	A
O	D	C	O	B	A	L	T

HOW CAN YOU DESTROY A MAGNET?

AIM 16 | How can you destroy a magnet?

Do you remember what happens when a magnetic substance becomes a magnet? The atoms group together. They become domains and line up. All the north poles face one way. All south poles face the other way. Its magnetic power is felt because the domains work together. They pull in only one direction.

What would happen if the domains faced in many directions? The magnet would grow weak. It would lose its magnetic power.

How do you make the domains go out of line? Here are three ways:

HAMMERING

When you hammer a magnet, the domains go out of line. When you stop hammering, the domains do not line up again. The magnet is weakened or destroyed.

HEATING RED HOT

When you heat a magnet until it is red hot, all the domains are upset. When the metal cools, the domains do not go back in line. The magnet loses all its power.

STROKING BACK AND FORTH

To make a magnet by stroking, you stroke the magnetic substance many times in one direction with a magnet.

But if you stroke the magnet back and forth with another magnet, the domains move out of line. They do not go back when the stroking stops.

A magnet can be made and destroyed over and over again.

WHAT DO THE PICTURES SHOW?

Look at each picture. Then answer the questions.

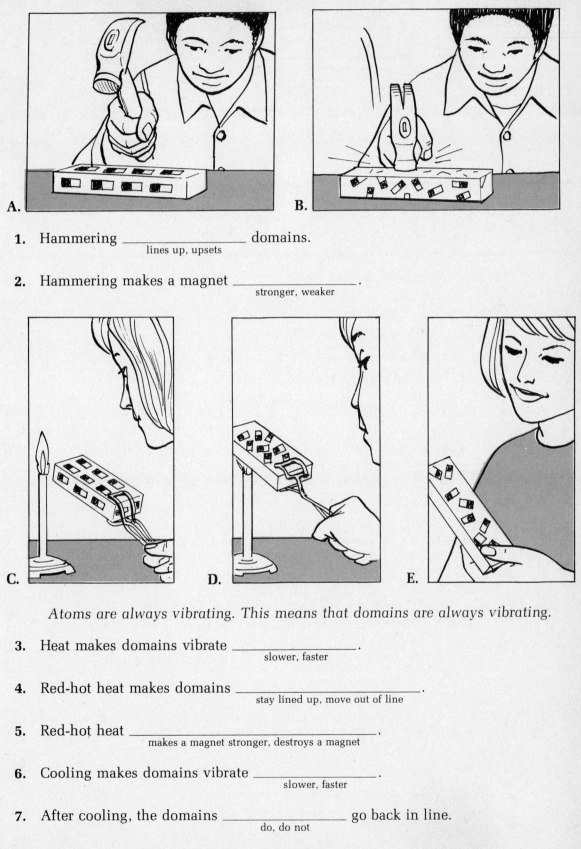

A.

B.

1. Hammering _____ domains.

                          lines up, upsets

2. Hammering makes a magnet _____.

                                            stronger, weaker

C.

D.

E.

Atoms are always vibrating. This means that domains are always vibrating.

3. Heat makes domains vibrate _____.

                                slower, faster

4. Red-hot heat makes domains _____.

                                    stay lined up, move out of line

5. Red-hot heat _____.

                              makes a magnet stronger, destroys a magnet

6. Cooling makes domains vibrate _____.

                                      slower, faster

7. After cooling, the domains _____ go back in line.

                                do, do not

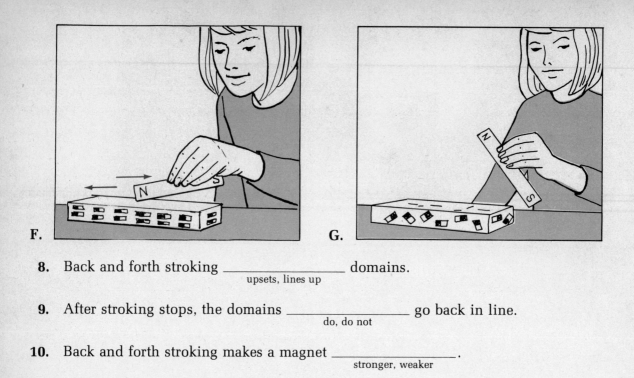

F.

G.

8. Back and forth stroking _____ domains.
upsets, lines up

9. After stroking stops, the domains _____ go back in line.
do, do not

10. Back and forth stroking makes a magnet _____.
stronger, weaker

TRUE OR FALSE   Write T on the line next to the number if the sentence is true. Write F if the sentence is false.

1. _____ Hammering a magnet lines up the domains.

2. _____ Hammering can destroy a magnet.

3. _____ Atoms move only when they are heated.

4. _____ Atoms move faster when they are heated.

5. _____ Heating a magnet red-hot makes a magnet stronger.

6. _____ After you heat a magnet red-hot, the domains do not go back in line.

7. _____ Stroking a magnet in one direction with another magnet destroys the magnet.

8. _____ Stroking a magnet back and forth with another magnet upsets the domains.

FILL-IN QUESTIONS

Fill in the correct answer for each of the following:

1. List three ways to destroy a magnet. _____ _____

   _____

2. What happens to the domains when a magnet is destroyed? _____

   _____

MULTIPLE CHOICE

On the space on the right, write the letter that best completes each sentence.

1. You can destroy a magnet by   1. _____
   a) contact.
   b) stroking in one direction with another magnet.
   c) hammering it.

2. Heat makes atoms vibrate   2. _____
   a) faster.
   b) slower.
   c) at the same speed.

3. Red-hot heat makes domains   3. _____
   a) line up.
   b) go out of line.
   c) move slower.

4. Stroking a magnet back and forth with another magnet   4. _____
   a) makes the magnet stronger.
   b) makes the magnet weaker.
   c) does not change the magnet.

5. Stroking a magnet with copper   5. _____
   a) always
   b) sometimes
   c) never
   destroys the magnet.

MATCHING

Match the two lists. Write the correct letter on the line next to each number.

1. _____ domain

2. _____ heating red hot, hammering, stroking back and forth with another magnet

3. _____ magnetic field

4. _____ vibrate

5. _____ atoms

a) ways of destroying a magnet

b) to shake rapidly

c) group of lined-up atoms

d) always vibrating

e) area of magnetic energy

WORD SCRAMBLE

Unscramble each of the following words to form a word or term that you have read in this Aim.

1. RAMHEM _____

2. TENHAGI _____

3. GRITKONS _____

4. TAGMEN _____

HOW DOES A COMPASS WORK?

17

compass: an instrument that tells direction

geographic poles: the area of the earth around which the earth turns

magnetic poles: the north and south centers of the earth's magnetic field

AIM 17 | How does a compass work?

Long ago, sailors made an important discovery. They held a string with a piece of magnetite tied to it. No matter which way the ship turned, the same end of the magnetite always pointed north. This was the first compass. It helped sailors find their way when they could not see land. It helped when the sun or the stars were hidden by clouds.

A compass still helps us find our way. Every ship and airplane has one. Maybe you have used one—on a hike or in a boat.

Our compasses are not made of magnetite on a string. A modern compass has a *pointer* or *needle*. The pointer is a thin permanent magnet. It rests on a sharp point so it can turn easily.

How does a compass work?

A compass needle acts like any magnet. It is attracted to an unlike pole of another magnet and repelled by a like pole.

How does a compass find direction?

The earth is like a very large but weak magnet. It has a north pole, a south pole, and a magnetic field.

The earth's magnetic field pulls on the compass needle —it makes it turn. One end of the needle points north; the other end points south.

Don't get mixed up! The *north magnetic pole* and the *south magnetic pole* are not in exactly the same places as the geographic North Pole and South Pole.

WHAT DO THE PICTURES SHOW?

Look at each picture. Then answer the questions.

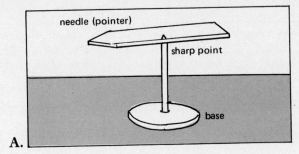

A.

A COMPASS

B.

C.

A compass needle acts like any magnet—it is attracted to an unlike pole of another magnet

and repelled by a like pole.

1. Which pole of the needle is closest to the magnet in Figure **B**? _____

2. Which pole of the needle is closest to the magnet in Figure **C**? _____

3. Which has a stronger magnetic field, the earth or the magnet? _____

A compass pointer is shaped like an *arrow* or a *diamond*.

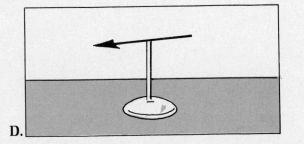

D.

E.

4. Pointer **D** is shaped like _____.
   _{an arrow, a diamond}

5. The tip points _____.
   _{north, south}

6. Pointer **E** is shaped like _____.
   _{an arrow, a diamond}

105

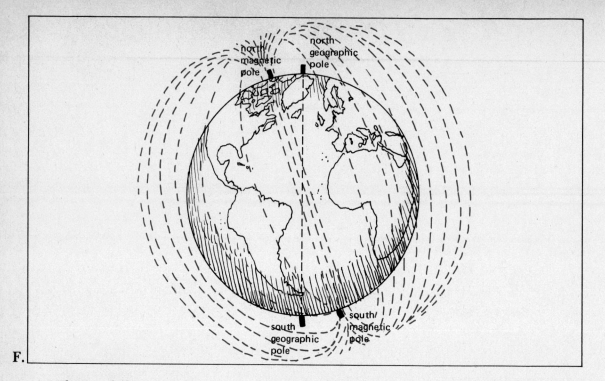

F.

The earth has two kinds of north and south poles; the *magnetic* poles and the *geographic* poles.

They are not in the same places.

The earth *spins* around its geographic poles.

A compass needle points to the *magnetic* poles.

TRUE OR FALSE   Write T on the line next to the number if the sentence is true. Write F if the sentence is false.

1. _____ A magnet makes a compass needle turn.

2. _____ A magnetic field makes a compass needle turn.

3. _____ The earth has a magnetic field.

4. _____ A compass needle *always* points north and south, even near a magnet.

5. _____ A compass needle is a permanent magnet.

6. _____ A compass needle is made of soft iron.

7. _____ The geographic poles are the same as the magnetic poles.

8. _____ A compass needle points to geographic north.

FILL-IN QUESTIONS

FILL-IN Fill in the correct answer for each of the following.
QUESTIONS

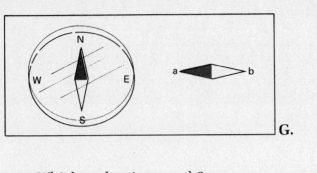

G.

1. Which end points north? _____
    a, b

2. Which end points south? _____
    a, b

3. A compass tells direction because the earth acts like a very large _____.

4. Is the earth's magnetic field strong or weak? _____

5. A compass is placed near a magnet. The needle will turn to _____

    _____.
    the earth's magnetic pole, the magnet

6. A magnetic needle *pivots* on a sharp point. What do you think the word "pivot"

    means? _____

7. Before the compass was discovered, sailors found their way by using _____

    _____.
    the stars, arrows

8. In outer space, a compass _____ be used to tell direction.
    can, cannot

MATCHING Match the two lists. Write the correct letter on the line next to each number.

1. _____ earth   **a)** points north and south

2. _____ compass needle   **b)** not in the same place

3. _____ small piece of magnetite   **c)** the points around which the earth
    on a string   rotates

4. _____ geographic poles   **d)** huge but weak magnet

5. _____ magnetic and   **e)** early compass
    geographic poles

LIVING COMPASSES

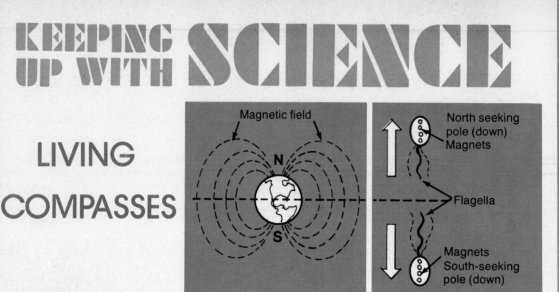

Suppose you were blindfolded. You could not see a compass, the sun, the stars, or any familiar thing. Would you "know" where north or south is? You wouldn't! You couldn't! Without outside help, humans have no way of knowing direction. People have no built-in compasses.

Some bacteria, however, do have just that — built-in compasses. These compasses let the bacteria align themselves with the earth's magnetic field.

Why would bacteria want to know where north or south is? Bacteria, like all living things, need food. Bacteria without compasses cannot tell up and down. They just float around.

But bacteria are better off if they can swim down. "Down" is where food is—in the bottom sediment. Self-moving bacteria have tiny tails called *flagella*. The bacteria move by whipping the flagella.

There is a relationship between north and south and up and down. In the Northern Hemisphere *down is north*. In the Southern Hemisphere *down is south*.

Recently it has been discovered that the flagella of magnetic bacteria found in the Northern Hemisphere are *opposite the north seeking pole* of their built-in compasses. Therefore, the flagella moves the bacteria towards the north —*which is*

down.

The flagella of magnetic bacteria found in the Southern Hemisphere are *opposite to the south seeking pole* of their built-in compasses. Therefore, the flagella propel the bacteria towards the *south— which is also down.*

Near the equator, however, the earth's magnetic field is not up nor down. It is *horizontal*. Therefore, bacteria cannot find "down" by lining up with the earth's magnetic field. What do you suppose? So far, *no magnetic bacteria have been found near the equator.*

Bacteria "grow" their internal magnets from iron they take in from water.

Bacteria are not the only organisms that produce internal magnets. Magnetic iron has been found in the skulls of pigeons and in the stomachs of bees. Do these internal magnets help pigeons find their way home? Do they influence where bees build their hives? Do they help them find their way back to the hive? Scientists do not yet know. But these questions are being studied.

The discovery of magnetic bacteria has opened an interesting new field of scientific study. Do higher organisms contain magnetic iron? If so, how do these built-in compasses influence their behavior?

WHAT IS AN ELECTROMAGNET?

18

electromagnet: a temporary magnet made by using electrical current

AIM 18 | What is an electromagnet?

Many important discoveries are made by accident. One of these discoveries was made by a Danish schoolteacher.

In 1819, Hans Oersted [UR sted] put a compass near an electric circuit. *The compass needle turned toward the wire.* Oersted turned off the electric current. The compass needle turned back to where it had been.

Oersted tried it again and again. The same thing happened each time. He knew that only a magnetic field can turn a compass needle. *The magnetic field that turned the needle could have come only from the electricity!*

Oersted had shown that *an electric current gives off a magnetic field.* This discovery led to many useful inventions. One of these inventions is the *electromagnet.* An electromagnet is a temporary magnet. It gets its magnetism from electricity. When the electricity stops, the magnetism stops. An electromagnet has many important uses.

Three things are needed to make an electromagnet:

1. a soft iron core
2. a coil of insulated wire
3. a source of electricity.

A switch is helpful, but not necessary.

When you connect the parts, electricity moves through the wire. The electricity creates a magnetic field. The field magnetizes the core by induction. When the electricity stops, the core loses its magnetism.

WHAT DO THE PICTURES SHOW?

Look at each picture. Then answer the questions.

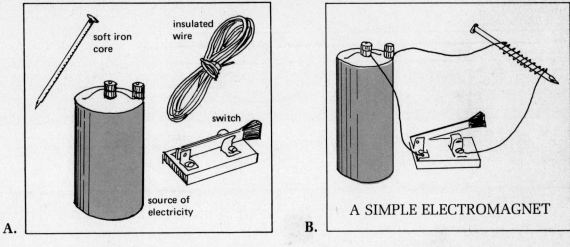

A.

B. A SIMPLE ELECTROMAGNET

I.

1. Which of the parts in Figure **A** must an electromagnet have? _____

   _____

2. Which part is helpful, but not necessary? _____

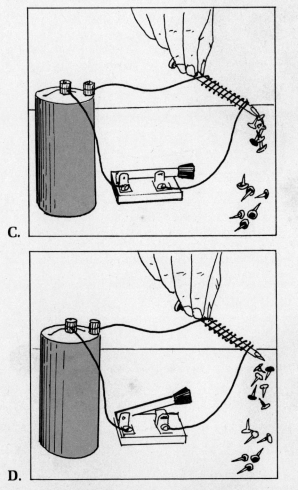

C.

D.

II.

3. This circuit is _____.

complete, incomplete

4. Electricity _____ mov-

is, is not
   ing through the wire.

5. The iron core _____

has, has not
   become a magnet.

6. If you open the switch, the tacks

   _____.

drop, do not drop

7. An electromagnet is a

   _____ magnet.

temporary, permanent

111

OERSTED'S EXPERIMENT

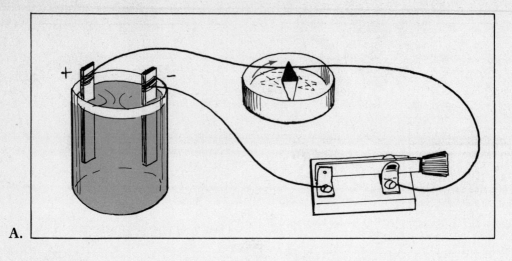

A.

I. Oersted placed a compass near an electric circuit. The needle turned.

1. The compass needle turned _____ the wire.
   towards, away from

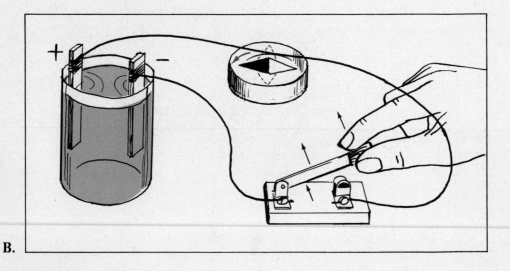

B.

II. Oersted turned off the current. The needle turned back to where it had been.

Oersted tried this over and over again. The same thing happened each time.

When the current was on, the compass needle pointed towards the wire. When the current was shut off, the needle turned back again.

2. What made the compass needle turn? _____

   Where did the magnetic field come from? _____

3. What did Oersted prove? _____

_____

COMPLETING SENTENCES

Complete the sentences with the words below.

magnet	temporary	coil of insulated wire
soft iron core	compass	electromagnet
induction	magnetic field	source of electricity

1. Hans Oersted found out that electricity gives off a _____.

2. Magnetic energy makes iron become a _____.

3. Iron can become only a _____ magnet.

4. An _____ is a temporary magnet.

5. An electromagnet becomes a magnet by _____.

6. To make an electromagnet, you need: a _____, a _____,

   and a _____.

7. A _____ can tell us if electricity is moving through a wire.

TRUE OR FALSE

Write T on the line next to the number if the sentence is true. Write F if the sentence is false.

1. _____ Permanent means lasting a very long time.

2. _____ An electromagnet is a permanent magnet.

3. _____ Soft iron loses its magnetism easily.

4. _____ Steel loses its magnetism easily.

5. _____ The core of an electromagnet is soft iron.

6. _____ When an electromagnet is connected, the core has a north and south pole.

7. _____ A magnetic field surrounds every wire.

8. _____ A compass turns when it is near any electrical wire.

} Careful these are tricky!

9. _____ A temporary magnet can be switched on and off.

10. _____ A permanent magnet can be switched on and off.

113

1. _____ soft iron core, coil of insulated wire, source of electricity

2. _____ magnetic field

3. _____ steel

4. _____ compass

5. _____ Oersted

a) turns towards magnetic field

b) parts of an electromagnet

c) discovered that electricity gives off magnetism

d) not good as electromagnet core

e) given off by electricity

THROW ONE OUT! In each of the following sets of terms, one of the terms does *not* belong. Circle that term.

1. switch open   magnetic field   electricity moving

2. switch closed   no magnetic field   no electricity flowing

3. electromagnet   soft iron core   steel core

4. electromagnet   permanent magnet   temporary magnet

5. compass   magnetic pole   geographic pole

WHAT MAKES AN ELECTROMAGNET STRONGER?

19

AIM 19 | What makes an electromagnet stronger?

You may have seen an electromagnet in a junk yard. It is *huge*. It lifts whole cars. Inside your telephone is a *tiny* electromagnet. It lets you hear people speak. The huge electromagnet in the junk yard is strong. The tiny electromagnet in your telephone is weak. Electromagnets of different strengths are needed for different jobs.

Weak electromagnets do small jobs. Strong electromagnets do big jobs. The stronger an electromagnet is, the more work it can do.

When an electromagnet is made, the designer thinks about the job it must do. Then the correct size is made for the job.

How can you make an electromagnet *stronger*? There are three ways:

1. Wind more wire around the coil.
2. Use a stronger electric current.
3. Use a larger core.

There is a limit to how strong an electromagnet can be made. The core can be "filled" with magnetism. Then it cannot be made stronger.

Try the experiment on the next page. You will see for yourself how an electromagnet can be made stronger.

EXPERIMENTING WITH ELECTROMAGNETS

What You Need   two 1½-volt dry cells
two large iron nails
insulated wire
switch
small steel tacks

How To Do the Experiment

1. Hook up your electromagnet. The chart below shows six different ways.
2. Test each hook up.

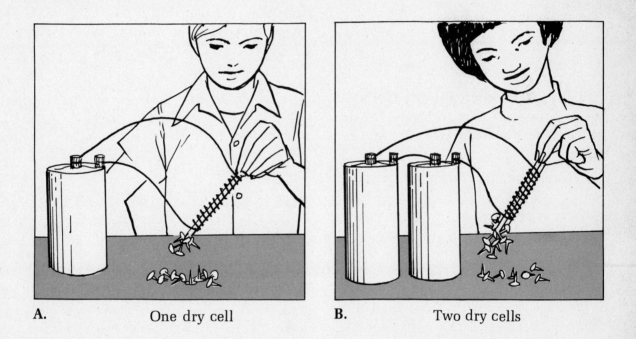

A.   One dry cell   **B.**   Two dry cells

Count how many tacks the electromagnet lifts. Write the numbers on the chart.

	Number of Wire Turns	Number of Dry Cells	Number of Cores (Nails)	Number of Tacks Picked Up
1.	20	1	1	
2.	40	1	1	
3.	20	2	1	
4.	20	1	2	
5.	40	2	1	
6.	40	2	2	

What You Learned

1. More wire turns make an electromagnet _____.
    stronger, weaker

2. Stronger voltage makes an electromagnet _____.
    stronger, weaker

3. A larger core makes an electromagnet _____.
    stronger, weaker

4. Fewer wire turns make an electromagnet _____.
    stronger, weaker

5. Weaker voltage makes an electromagnet _____.
    stronger, weaker

6. A smaller core makes an electromagnet _____.
    stronger, weaker

ANSWER THESE QUESTIONS

1. An electromagnet is a _____ magnet.
    temporary, permanent

2. Name the three important parts of an electromagnet.

    _____ _____ _____

3. What kind of metal is used as the core of an electromagnet? _____

4. List three ways to make an electromagnet stronger.

    _____

    _____

    _____

HOW CAN YOU USE A MAGNET TO MAKE ELECTRICITY?

20

AIM 20 | How can you use a magnet to make electricity?

Magnetism and electricity are *not* the same. But they are *related*. You have learned that electricity gives off magnetic energy. The opposite is also true—*magnetism gives off electric energy*.

Michael Faraday [FA ruh day] was a British scientist. In 1831, he learned that magnetic energy can be used to make electricity. Faraday tried two experiments:

1. He moved a permanent magnet back and forth inside a coil of insulated wire. This produced an electric current.
2. Then he moved the coil back and forth around the magnet. Again, he produced an electric current.

Faraday had made the first electric generator. It was a simple generator. It produced weak electricity. But it *was* a generator.

How does a generator make electricity? Magnetic lines of force surround every magnet. Movement through the lines of force is called *breaking* or *cutting* the lines of force. If a coil of insulated wire breaks the lines of force, electrons in the wire move. That means electricity is produced. We can measure weak electrical current with a galvanometer.

There are two ways of breaking the lines of force: 1] move the coil or 2] move the magnet.

In most generators, the coil moves. It turns between the poles of a permanent magnet. If the coil turns faster—or if a stronger magnet is used—you get a stronger electrical current.

Giant generators are needed to make all our electricity.

WHAT DOES THE PICTURE SHOW?

Look at the picture. Then answer the questions.

A.

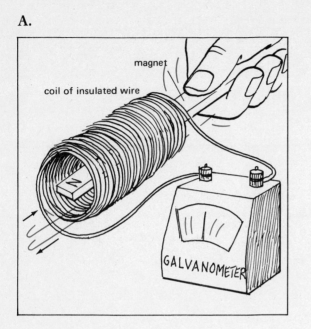

magnet

coil of insulated wire

GALVANOMETER

1. The instrument that is *making* electricity is called a _____.
   generator, galvanometer

2. **a)** The instrument that is *measuring* the electricity is called a _____.
   generator, galvanometer

   b) This instrument measures _____ electricity.
   strong, weak

3. In this simple generator, the _____ is moving.
   magnet, coil

4. If the coil would move instead, the electricity would _____.
   stop, be the same

5. If you move the coil or magnet slower, you get _____ electricity.
   stronger, weaker

6. If you move the coil or magnet faster, you get _____ electricity.
   stronger, weaker

7. If you use a stronger magnet, you get _____ electricity.
   stronger, weaker

8. If you use a weaker magnet, you get _____ electricity.
   stronger, weaker

Inside A Generator

The turning coil "breaks" the lines of force of the magnet.

This makes electricity move through the wire.

B.

permanent magnet

coil

121

COMPLETING SENTENCES

Complete the sentences with the choices below. One of these words may be used twice.

move   Faraday   permanent magnet
electricity   magnetic energy   galvanometer
turn the coil faster   weak   generator
coil of insulated wire use a stronger magnet

1. Electricity gives off _____.

2. Magnetic energy can be used to make _____.

3. The English scientist named _____ found out that magnetism can be used to make electricity.

4. The machine that makes electricity is called a _____.

5. The necessary parts of an electric generator are a _____ and a

   _____.

6. To make electricity, either the wire or the magnet must _____.

7. In most generators, the _____ moves.

8. A _____ measures weak electricity.

9. Weak magnets can make only _____ electricity.

10. Two ways to make stronger electricity are _____ and _____

    _____.

MATCHING

Match the two lists. Write the correct letter on the line next to each number.

1. _____ Michael Faraday   a) made first generator

2. _____ magnet and coil of   b) discovered that electricity gives
            insulated wire   magnetic energy

3. _____ galvanometer   c) measures weak voltage

4. _____ electricity   d) parts of a generator

5. _____ Oersted   e) moving electrons

TRUE OR FALSE

Write T on the line next to the number if the sentence is true. Write F if the sentence is false.

1. _____ A generator *needs* electricity to work.

2. _____ A generator *makes* electricity.

3. _____ We get electricity only from generators.

4. _____ Most of our electricity comes from generators.

5. _____ A generator must have a magnet.

6. _____ A generator must have a coil of insulated wire.

7. _____ A magnet and coil always give electricity.

8. _____ A magnet gives off electric energy.

9. _____ A magnet can make electrons move.

10. _____ Electricity is moving electrons.

FILL-IN QUESTIONS

Fill in the correct answer for each of the following. (Turn back to previous Aims if necessary).

1. List the three necessary parts of an electromagnet. _____

_____

2. Name the part of an electromagnet that is useful but not necessary. _____

_____

3. Who discovered that electricity gives off magnetism? _____

4. What kind of magnet is an electromagnet? _____

5. List the three ways to make an electromagnet stronger. _____

_____

6. Can an electromagnet be made stronger and stronger without stopping? _____

_____

7. List two uses of the electromagnet. _____

8. What did Michael Faraday discover? _____

9. Name the machine that makes electricity. _____

10. List the important parts of a generator. _____

WORD SCRAMBLE

Unscramble each of the following to form a word or term that you have read in this Aim.

1. TENRAGREO _____

2. GATMEN _____

3. LOIC _____

4. LOVGATE _____

5. TRUNREC _____

REACHING OUT

Water power turns the coils of some generators. What are some other ways to turn the coil?

_____

_____

_____

_____

HOW DOES A GENERATOR COIL TURN?

21

AIM 21 | How does a generator coil turn?

Electricity is a form of energy. It can make things move.

A generator produces electricity. Its coil turns between the poles of a permanent magnet. But what turns the coil?

Any form of energy can turn a generator coil. Even wind can be used. But wind is not reliable. Wind does not blow all the time. And, in most places, it does not blow very hard. At best, wind produces only small amounts of electricity.

Swift-moving water is a reliable way to produce electricity. Places like Niagara Falls have huge generators. They produce electricity for hundreds of thousands of people.

Dams also produce large amounts of electricity. A dam stores water. When the water is let out, it turns generator coils.

Places with powerful waterfalls or dams are important in producing electricity. But most places do not have falls or dams. Most electricity is produced by steam power. Fuels, like coal, oil, and gas, boil water. Boiling water produces steam. The force of the steam turns generator coils.

Some energy for making electricity comes from atomic fuel.

Atomic energy and fuel burning have a serious problem —they pollute. Coal, oil, and gas burning gives off unwanted gases. Burning coal also gives off solid wastes. Atomic energy gives off dangerous radiation. There is also a danger of an atomic explosion. Thousands of people can die.

Scientists are trying to find cheap and "clean" ways to produce electricity.

ENERGY FOR GENERATORS

A.

B.

C.

In Figure A the energy of wind is spinning the blades, which turn the coils of a generator.

1. Does wind blow all the time in most places? _____

2. Does wind always blow hard?

   _____

3. Is wind energy a reliable way of producing electricity? _____

Figure B shows a waterfall. Swift-moving water is spinning the turbines, which turn the coils of the generators.

4. Will there always be moving water here? _____

5. Is swift-moving water a reliable way of producing electricity? ____

   _____

Figure C shows a dam with turbines and generators.

6. How is Figure C different from Figure B? _____

7. Do wind and moving water give off pollution? _____

D.

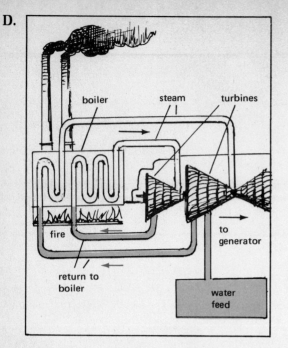

The energy of steam is spinning the turbines, which turn the coils of the generator.

8. **a)** Name three kinds of fuels we burn to make steam.

_____

_____

_____

b) What other kind of energy produces a _great_ amount of heat.

_____

9. Does burning fuel give off pollution?

_____

10. **a)** What kind of pollution do coal, oil, and gas give off?

_____

b) What other kind of pollution does coal give off?

_____

11. **a)** Does atomic energy pollute? _____

b) What kind of pollution does atomic energy give off? _____

c) Is this the only danger in using atomic energy? _____

d) What other danger is there? _____

E.

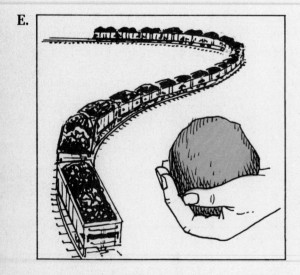

COMPARING COAL ENERGY WITH ATOMIC ENERGY

Just .45 kilograms (1 lb) of uranium (atomic fuel) gives the same energy as 1,043,262 kilograms (2,300,000 lbs) of coal.

This much coal would fill about 20 freight cars.

COMPLETING SENTENCES

Complete the sentences with the choices below. Two of these may be used twice.

coil of insulated wire   cannot   coal
gas   generator   swift-moving water
steam   oil   permanent magnet
move   wind   atomic
pollution

1. Electricity is made with a _____.

2. The two important parts of a generator are a _____ and a

 _____.

3. In a generator, either the coil or the magnet must _____.

4. In most generators, the _____ turns.

5. Three forces that can turn a generator coil are _____, _____,

 and _____.

6. We _____ rely upon wind to produce electricity.

7. Boiling water produces _____.

8. Three fuels we burn to produce steam are _____, _____,

 and _____.

9. The energy that gives the greatest heat is _____ energy.

10. Atomic energy and burning fuels create _____.

MATCHING

Match the two lists. Write the correct letter on the line next to each number.

1. _____ generator

2. _____ pollution

3. _____ coal, oil, gas

4. _____ atomic energy

5. _____ dam

a) unwanted things

b) radiation danger

c) holds water

d) machine that produces electricity

e) fuels

KEEPING UP WITH SCIENCE

PLUGGING

INTO

THE SUN

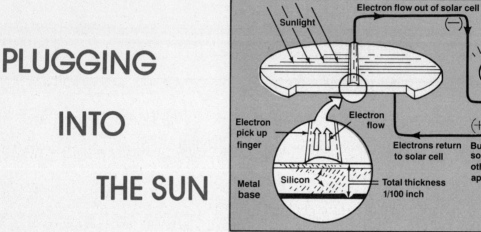

Scientists have discovered a way of turning sunlight directly into electricity. It is called *photovoltaics*.

Photovoltaics depends upon the *solar cell*. Today's solar cell is made of a slice of a single silicon crystal placed upon a very thin metal base. The base is laced with micro-thin wires. Each cell is about 3 to 6 inches in diameter (or smaller) and is thinner than a human hair.

When sunlight strikes the silicon atoms of a solar cell, their electrons are pushed into the wires. The moving electrons are an *electric current*. After the electrons do their job, such as lighting a bulb, they return to their silicon atoms in the solar cell. They are now ready to be pumped out again...and again. A solar cell can work without stopping for 30 years.

Solar cells have been used mainly for special jobs like powering satellites. Today, you can buy solar-powered watches, pocket calculators, and even portable radios. These require only weak electric currents.

Why don't we use photovoltaic elec-

tricity for bigger everyday jobs—like lighting our homes or running factory motors? The answer, in one word, is MONEY. In its present form, photovoltaic electricity is too expensive. A single solar cell produces only a very weak current. Much stronger currents are needed to power a home or factory. To achieve this power, many solar cells must be bunched together. And they are still costly. At present you would need $12,000 worth of solar cells to power an ordinary toaster.

Looks bad for photovoltaics? Not at all! Scientists are rapidly developing ways to bring down the cost greatly. By the year 2000, solar cells are expected to supply 20 percent of our nation's electricity.

However, solar cells need help. At night, no solar electricity is produced. On cloudy days, the electric output is reduced to almost nothing. Batteries can help at these times. But battery technology must be greatly improved. Batteries could store solar-cell electricity during peak sun hours. Regular generator-produced electricity can also be used.

WHAT IS A TRANSFORMER?

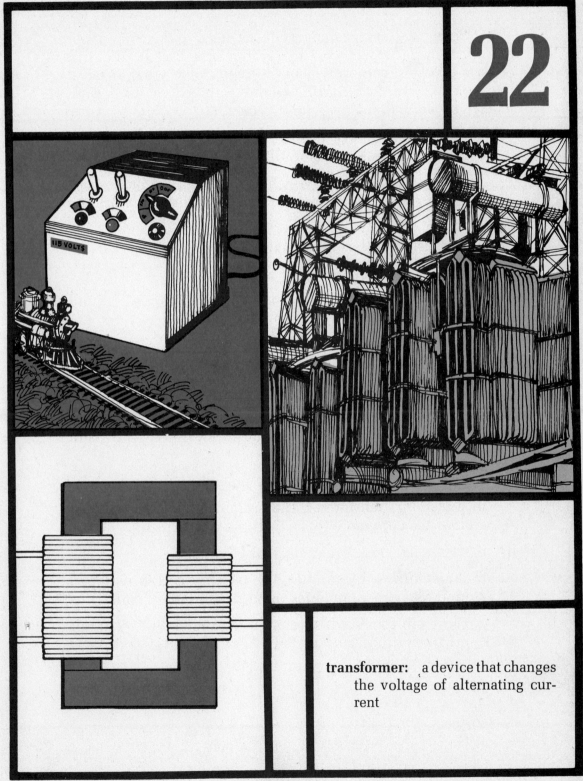

transformer: a device that changes the voltage of alternating current

AIM 22 | What is a transformer?

Some electric passenger trains need huge electromotive force to turn their wheels—as much as 11,000 volts. An electric toy train uses only about 18 volts. The wires in most homes carry about 115 volts. Some appliances need high voltage to work. Some need low voltage.

Sometimes voltage must be made stronger; sometimes it must be made weaker to suit different devices.

How can we change voltage? By using a *transformer*. There are large and small transformers. But they all work the same way.

A transformer has three main parts: (Figure A).

- a soft iron core, and
- *two* different coils of insulated wire wrapped around the core.

One of these coils is called the *primary coil*. The primary coil is connected to the *electricity* coming in.

The other coil is called the *secondary coil*. The secondary coil is connected to the *appliance*.

There are two kinds of transformers—*step-up*, and *step-down*.

I. A *step-up* transformer *increases* voltage.

In a *step-up* transformer, the secondary coil is wrapped around the core more times than the primary coil.

II. A *step-down* transformer *decreases* voltage.

In a *step-down* transformer, the primary coil is wrapped around the core more times than the secondary coil.

There are two kinds of electric current—*direct* current (DC) and *alternating* current (AC). Transformers work only with alternating current.

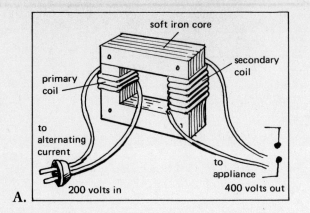

A. 200 volts in   400 volts out

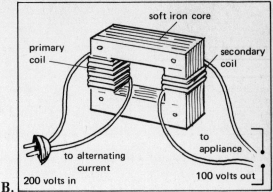

B. 200 volts in   100 volts out

This step-up transformer has *3* turns in the primary coil.

The secondary coil has *6* turns. This is twice the turns as the primary coil. It *doubles* the voltage.

For example: If you start out with 200 volts, you end up with *400* volts.

This step-down transformer has *6* turns in the primary coil.

The secondary coil has *3* turns. This is *one half* the turns as the primary coil. It makes the voltage *half* as strong.

For example: If you start out with 200 volts, you end up with *100* volts.

DIFFERENCES BETWEEN DIRECT CURRENT AND ALTERNATING CURRENT

In DIRECT CURRENT:

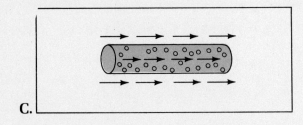

C.

In ALTERNATING CURRENT:

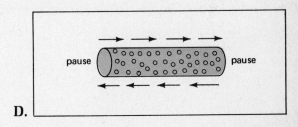

D.

a) The electricity moves through the circuit *in one direction only.*

b) It does *not* move back and forth.

c) Direct current does *not* stop and go, stop and go. *REMEMBER THIS.*

a) The electricity moves *back and forth* many times a second.

b) Each time the electricity changes direction, it *stops for a moment.* It happens very fast.

c) *Remember*—alternating current *stops* and *goes, stops* and *goes, stops* and *goes.*

A TRANSFORMER CHANGES ONLY ALTERNATING CURRENT

Most people all over the world use alternating current.

WORKING WITH TRANSFORMERS

Figures E and F show transformers. Study each one. Then answer the questions next to the figure.

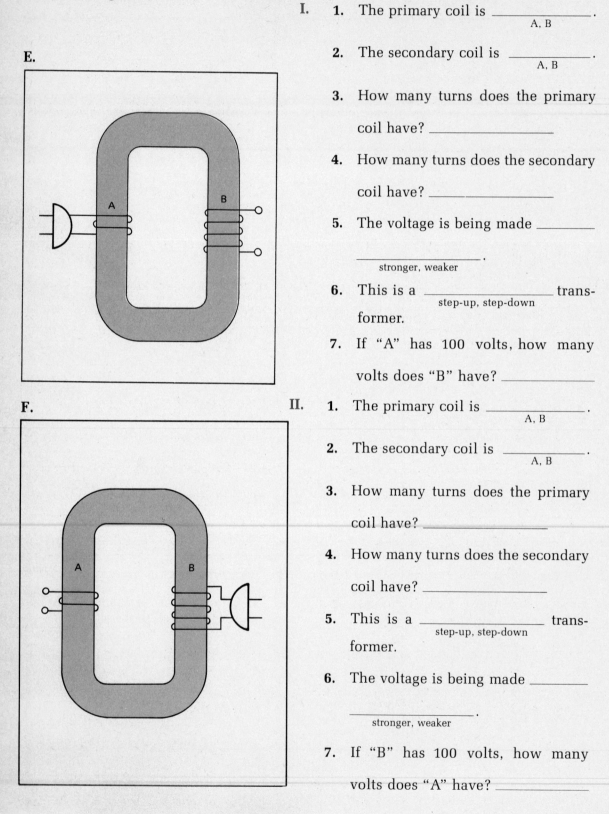

E.

F.

I.
1. The primary coil is _____.
   _{A, B}

2. The secondary coil is _____.
   _{A, B}

3. How many turns does the primary coil have? _____

4. How many turns does the secondary coil have? _____

5. The voltage is being made _____
   _____.
   stronger, weaker

6. This is a _____ trans-
   step-up, step-down
   former.

7. If "A" has 100 volts, how many volts does "B" have? _____

II.
1. The primary coil is _____.
   _{A, B}

2. The secondary coil is _____.
   _{A, B}

3. How many turns does the primary coil have? _____

4. How many turns does the secondary coil have? _____

5. This is a _____ trans-
   step-up, step-down
   former.

6. The voltage is being made _____
   _____.
   stronger, weaker

7. If "B" has 100 volts, how many volts does "A" have? _____

G.

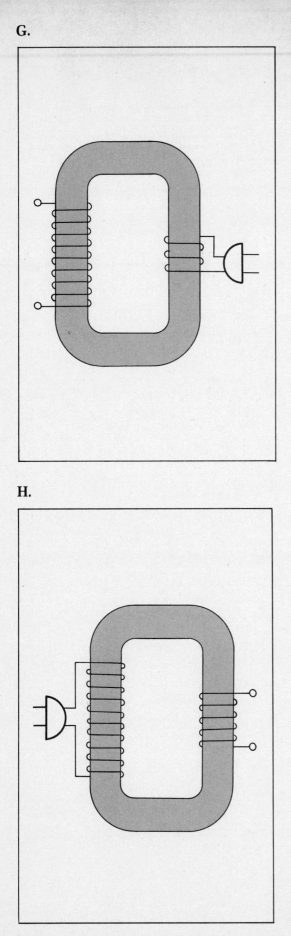

III. **1.** How many turns are there

    a) in the primary coil? _____

    b) in the secondary coil? _____

2. The primary coil is connected to the

    _____ .
    _{electric current, appliance}

3. The secondary coil is connected to

    the _____ .
            _{electric current, appliance}

4. This is a _____ trans-
              _{step-up, step-down}

    former.

5. The voltage is being made

    _____ .
      _{stronger, weaker}

6. If the primary coil has 100 volts, how many volts does the secondary

    coil have? _____

H.

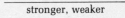

IV. **1.** How many turns are there

    a) in the primary coil? _____

    b) in the secondary coil? _____

2. The primary coil is connected to the

    _____ .
        _{electric current, appliance}

3. The secondary coil is connected to

    the _____ .
            _{electric current, appliance}

4. This is a _____ trans-
              _{step-up, step-down}

    former.

5. The voltage is being made

    _____ .
      _{stronger, weaker}

6. If the primary coil has 100 volts, how many volts does the secondary

    coil have? _____

135

Complete the sentences with the choices below. One of these may be used twice.

---

two coils of insulated wire   step-up   without stopping
stops and goes   direct   weaker
step-down   soft iron core   transformer
alternating   stronger

1. There are two kinds of electric currents. They are _____ current, and

    _____ current.

2. Direct current moves _____.

3. Alternating current _____ many times every second.

4. A _____ changes voltage.

5. A transformer works only with _____ current.

6. The important parts of a transformer are: a _____ and

    _____.

7. A step-up transformer makes voltage _____.

8. A step-down transformer makes voltage _____.

9. A _____ transformer has more turns in the secondary coil than in the primary coil.

10. A _____ transformer has more turns in the primary coil than in the secondary coil.

MATCHING Match the two lists. Write the correct letter on the line next to each number.

---

1. _____ step-up transformer

2. _____ step-down transformer

3. _____ soft iron core and two sets of coils

4. _____ soft iron

5. _____ alternating current

a) important parts of a transformer

b) makes voltage stronger

c) stops and goes many times a second

d) makes voltage weaker

e) transformer core

Write T on the line next to the number if the sentence is true. Write F if the sentence is false.

1. _____ A transformer changes amperes.

2. _____ The core of a transformer is made of steel.

3. _____ The primary coil of a transformer is connected to the appliance.

4. _____ The secondary coil of a transformer is connected to the appliance.

5. _____ A transformer only raises voltage.

6. _____ A step-up transformer makes voltage stronger.

7. _____ A step-down transformer makes voltage weaker.

8. _____ Direct current starts and stops many times a second.

9. _____ Alternating current starts and stops many times a second.

10. _____ A transformer works only with alternating current.

REACHING OUT A powerhouse generator may produce more than 22,000 volts. Huge step-up transformers boost it to nearly 350,000 volts.

1. Why is the voltage raised so much? _____

_____

_____

2. What happens to the voltage before it reaches your home? _____

_____

_____

Working with charts

Complete the missing information. The first one has been filled in for you.

A.

	Step-up Transformer	Step-down Transformer	Primary Coil Turns	Secondary Coil Turns	Primary Coil Voltage	Secondary Coil Voltage
1.	✓		20	40	10	20
2.			30		20	40
3.			25	5	50	
4.				10	5	50
5.			10	2	50	

B.

	Step-up Transformer	Step-down Transformer	Primary Coil Turns	Secondary Coil Turns	Primary Coil Voltage	Secondary Coil Voltage
1.				60	100	300
2.			6	24		200
3.			4		5	25
4.			100		50	5
5.				50	300	30

WHAT IS AN INDUCTION COIL?

23

induction coil: a device that increases the voltage of direct current

AIM 23 | What is an induction coil?

Cars, trucks, and buses run on gasoline. But they also need electricity. Each one needs *about 20,000 volts!*

Most car batteries give only 12 volts. This is not nearly strong enough.

Why not use a transformer to raise the voltage? This sounds like a good idea, *but it won't work.* A transformer works only with *alternating* current. And a car battery gives only *direct* current. Something else is needed.

What can boost the voltage of direct current? We use an *induction coil.* An induction coil and a transformer are very much alike. Each one has

—a soft iron core, and
—two coils of insulated wire.

But there is one important difference. A transformer has *no* moving parts. An induction coil has an *extra* part that is *always moving.*

The extra part is a *switch* that opens and closes by itself many times a second. This makes the electricity stop-and-go, stop-and-go. The on-and-off switching makes the direct current *act* like alternating current. Because of this, the voltage can be changed.

The induction coil in a car can boost the 12 volts of the battery to 20,000 volts.

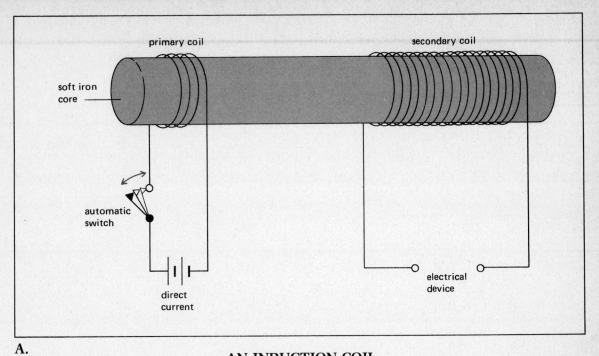

A.   **AN INDUCTION COIL**

COMPLETING SENTENCES Complete the sentences with the words below. Two of these words may be used three times.

direct current	alternating current	automatic switch
induction coil	direct	transformer
alternating		

1. There are two kinds of electricity; _____ current, and _____ current.

2. DC stands for _____.

3. AC stands for _____.

4. Electricity in schools and homes is usually _____ current.

5. _____ current moves without stopping.

6. _____ current starts and stops many times every second.

7. A _____ changes the voltage of alternating current.

8. An _____ changes the voltage of direct current.

9. Batteries give only _____ current.

10. The part that an induction coil has that a transformer does not have is an

   _____.

141

In each of the following sets of terms, one of the terms does *not* belong. Circle that term.

1. AC   DC   induction coil

2. AC   DC   home

3. toy electric trains   transformer   induction coil

4. more primary turns   more secondary turns   steps-up voltage

5. most used   AC   DC

**WORD
SEARCH** The words in the list are hidden in the group of letters. Try to find each word. Draw a line around the word. The spelling may go in any direction: up-and-down, across, or diagonally.

NORTH
SOUTH
INDUCTION
CORE
CURRENT
BATTERY
WIRE
COIL

H	S	O	E	B	C	U	T	N	H
P	D	E	C	A	H	T	U	O	S
W	N	O	I	T	C	U	D	N	I
R	I	W	E	T	O	T	N	O	W
L	N	R	I	E	R	S	U	R	H
W	C	U	R	R	E	N	T	T	O
C	I	E	W	Y	E	I	E	H	Y

**REACHING
OUT** An induction coil *can* make a flashlight burn brighter. Why is it not used?

_____

_____

_____

_____

WHAT IS HEAT?

24

vibrate: to move back and forth very fast

AIM 24 | What is heat?

Here is a trick question—Does an ice cube have heat? Think carefully! The answer is YES! An ice cube does have heat. It has less heat than water does. But it still has heat. *All matter has heat.* Some kinds of matter have more heat than other kinds.

WHAT IS HEAT?

Heat is a form of energy.

Heat is the energy of vibrating molecules — and molecules are always vibrating. This means that *all* matter has heat.

How hot an object is depends on how fast its molecules vibrate. The faster the molecules vibrate, the hotter the object is.

WHERE DOES HEAT COME FROM?

The *sun* provides most of our heat. The sun warms our earth. It makes plants and trees grow. Without the sun, we would have no food. And we need food to live.

Burning fuel provides some heat. Coal, oil, gas, and wood are some fuels that we burn. But without the sun, these fuels would not have formed.

Rubbing—or *friction*—also provides heat. Most heat that comes from friction is not wanted. For example, heat from friction can ruin machinery. Oil and grease help reduce friction.

LEARNING ABOUT HEAT

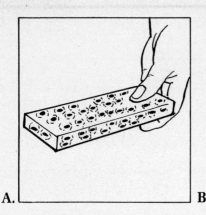

A.

Molecules are always vibrating.

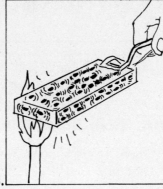

B.

Heat makes molecules vibrate faster.

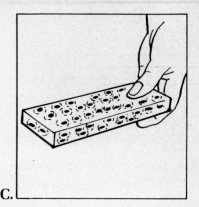

C.

When matter cools, its molecules vibrate slower.

SOURCES OF HEAT

D.

the sun

E.

burning fuel

F.

friction

The *atom* can give off a *tremendous* amount of heat. We are just learning how to use this heat.

In atomic (nuclear) power plants, certain kinds of atoms are bombarded and smashed. They give up energy in the form of heat. This heat changes water to steam. The steam turns the coils in generators, which produce electricity.

ENERGY CAN MAKE THINGS MOVE

There are many kinds of energy. Heat is one kind of energy. Heat can make things move.

A.

B.

Heat moves ocean liners, Diesel trucks—even your family car.

How does this happen?

1. Ocean liners, Diesel trucks, and automobile engines burn fuel.
2. Fuel has stored chemical energy. The chemical energy changes to heat energy.
3. The high temperature causes great pressure. The pressure causes movement.

C.

Heat has thousands of other uses too. For example, we use heat to warm our homes and to cook our food. Doctors use heat to kill germs. Heat is used to make metal products.

4. Heat is one form of energy. What other form of energy did you learn about in this

book? _____

Complete the sentences with the choices below. Three of these may be used twice.

---

electricity	more	vibrating molecules
sun	move	heat
vibrating	friction	less

1. Energy can make things _____.

2. Two kinds of energy are _____ and _____.

3. Heat is caused by _____.

4. All matter has _____ because molecules are always _____.

5. Warm matter has _____ heat than cold matter.

6. Cool matter has _____ heat than warm matter.

7. The faster molecules vibrate, the _____ heat they give off.

8. The slower molecules vibrate, the _____ heat they give off.

9. Most heat comes from the _____.

10. Rubbing produces heat. Another name for rubbing is _____.

TRUE OR FALSE Write T on the line next to the number if the sentence is true. Write F if the sentence is false.

---

1. _____ All molecules vibrate.

2. _____ Molecules always vibrate at the same speed.

3. _____ The faster molecules vibrate, the less heat they give off.

4. _____ Most of our heat comes from the moon.

5. _____ Coal, wood, oil, and gas are fuels.

6. _____ Without the sun, we would have no coal, wood, oil, or gas.

7. _____ A piece of dust has heat.

8. _____ A flame always gives off heat.

9. _____ Heat always gives off a flame.

MATCHING

Match the two lists. Write the correct letter on the line next to each number.

1. _____ friction   **a)** gives us most of our heat

2. _____ sun   **b)** examples of fuel

3. _____ vibrating molecules   **c)** can make things move

4. _____ energy   **d)** rubbing

5. _____ coal, wood, oil, gas   **e)** cause all heat

WORD SCRAMBLE

Unscramble each of the following to form a word or term that you have read in this Aim.

1. REGYEN   _____

2. LUFE   _____

3. TROCINIF   _____

4. TEAH   _____

5. BUNGBIR   _____

REACHING OUT

The boy is pumping air into the bike tire.

The pump is getting hot.

Can you explain why?

_____

_____

_____

_____

_____

HOW DOES HEAT CHANGE THE SIZE OF MATTER?

25

expand: to become larger

contract: to become smaller

AIM 25 | How does heat change the size of matter?

Household hint: If you cannot open the lid of a jar, hold the lid under hot water. Then unscrew the lid. Why does hot water work? The heat makes the lid a tiny bit *larger*. Then it is easier to turn.

HEAT MAKES THINGS LARGER.

Why? As you know, matter is made up of molecules that are always vibrating. The greater the heat, the *faster* they vibrate. When molecules vibrate faster, they need more room. They make more room by s–p–r–e–a–d–i–n–g o–u–t. The heated matter becomes larger. It *expands*.

When matter cools, the opposite happens. The molecules vibrate slower. Now they need less room. They move closer together. This makes the matter smaller. It contracts.

Most matter   expands when heated
                                and
                        contracts when cooled.

Temperature is always changing—growing warmer or cooler. The size of matter is always changing, too. Usually, matter expands or contracts only slightly. Size changes very little. Then it is not important. But sometimes, size changes a lot. Then it is very important. For example, when heat expands a roadway, the roadway can buckle. Heat expansion can make drawbridges stick.

Different kinds of matter expand at different rates. Some matter expands a great deal. Other matter expands only a little.

HOW DO HEAT AND COLD CHANGE THE SIZE OF MATTER?

I.   **How do heat and cold change the size of a *solid?***

What You Need   brass ring
brass ball that "just" fits through the ring
Bunsen burner
cold water

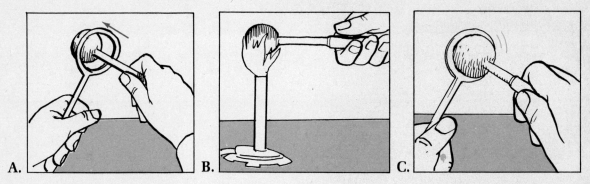

How To Do the Experiment

1.   Pass the brass ball through the ring. Notice the close fit (Figure **A**).

2.   Heat the ball over the flame for about one minute (Figure **B**).

3.   Now try to pass the ball through the ring (Figure **C**).

What You Saw; What You Learned

4.   The heated ball _____ pass through the ring.
did, did not

5.   The heat made the ball _____ .
smaller, larger

6.   The ball _____ .
expanded, contracted

Next Steps

7.   Dip the heated ball into the cold water(Figure **D**).

8.   Try to pass the ball through the ring(Figure **E**).

151

What You Saw; What You Learned

9. After the ball cooled, it _____ pass through the ring.
   did, did not

10. The cold water made the ball _____.
    smaller, larger

11. The ball _____.
    expanded, contracted

Conclusions

12. Heat _____ a solid.
    expands, contracts

13. Cold _____ a solid.
    expands, contracts

II. How do heat and cold change the size of a *liquid?*

What You Need

glass bottle
colored water
one-holed cork
glass tube
Bunsen burner

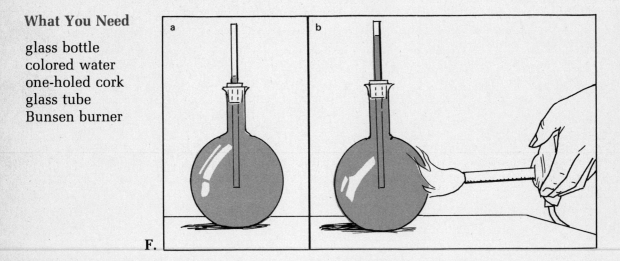

F.

How To Do the Experiment

1. Put colored water in the bottle. Cap with cork. Put glass tube through hole of cork and into the water.

2. Heat the bottle gently—just 3 or 4 seconds[Figure **F**]. Then take away the flame. [Watch the water level in the tube].

What You Saw; What You Learned

3. When you heated the bottle, the water in the tube moved _____.
   up, down

4. The water rose because it _____.
   expanded, contracted

152

5. When you took away the heat, the water became _____,
cooler, warmer

6. The water moved _____ in the tube.
up, down

7. The water moved down because it _____.
expanded, contracted

Conclusions

8. When a liquid is heated it _____.
expands, contracts

9. When a liquid cools, it _____.
expands, contracts

III. How do heat and cold change the size of *gas?*

What You Need

Pyrex bottle
colored water
one-holed cork
bulb-end glass tube
Bunsen burner

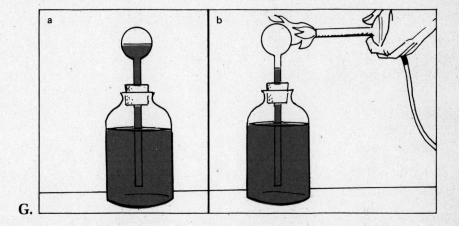

G.

What To Do

1. Set up equipment as shown (Figure **G**).

2. Heat *the bulb* gently—just 3 or 4 seconds (Figure **G**). Then take the flame away. (Watch the water level in the tube).

What You Saw: What You Learned

3. There is mostly _____ in the bulb.
water, gas

4. When you heated the bulb, the gas took up _____ room.
more, less

5. The gas _____.
expanded, contracted

6. The expanded gas _____.
made the water rise, pushed the water down

7. **a)** When you took away the heat, the gas _____ .
        became warmer, cooled a bit

    b) The gas _____ .
        expanded, contracted

    c) The gas pressed on the water with _____ force.
        more, less

    d) The water in the tube moved _____ .
        up, down

Conclusions

8. When a gas is heated, it _____ .
        expands, contracts

9. When a gas cools, it _____ .
        expands, contracts

You have learned that matter expands when heated and contracts when cooled. But *there are exceptions.*

One exception is *water.*

When water is cooled to make ice, it becomes bigger—*it expands.*

MATCHING   Match the two lists. Write the correct letter on the line next to each number.

1. _____ molecules   **a)** makes molecules vibrate faster

2. _____ heat   **b)** sun

3. _____ cold   **c)** always vibrating

4. _____ states of matter   **d)** solids, liquids, gases

5. _____ source of most heat **e)** makes molecules vibrate slower

Complete the sentences with the choices below. Two of these may be used twice.

---

expand	shake very rapidly	more
contracts	become smaller	become larger
heat	less	vibrating

1. *Vibrate* means to _____.

2. Molecules are always _____.

3. Vibrating molecules give off _____.

4. When molecules vibrate faster, they give off _____ heat.

5. When molecules vibrate faster, they need _____ room.

6. Heat makes matter _____ in size.
   (one word)

7. When molecules vibrate slower, they give off _____ heat.

8. When molecules vibrate slower, they need _____ room.

9. Matter that cools _____ in size.
   (one word)

10. *Expand* means _____; *contract* means _____.

Write T on the line next to the number if the sentence is true. Write F if the sentence is false.

---

1. _____ All molecules vibrate.

2. _____ The slower molecules vibrate, the more heat they give off.

3. _____ Matter contracts when it is heated.

4. _____ Matter contracts when it is cooled.

5. _____ All matter expands and contracts the same amount.

REACHING OUT

1. Why are there spaces along railroad tracks? _____

_____

2. Why do steel bridges have rollers or joints? _____

_____

3. Why are overhead wires hung with a slight sag in the summertime? _____

_____

4. Why are the same wires hung tightly during the wintertime? _____

_____

5. Why are sidewalks and roads made with "cracks"? _____

_____

6. Why are liquids never filled to the very top of a bottle? _____

_____

HOW DOES HEAT MOVE THROUGH SOLIDS?

26

conduction: the way heat moves through solids

AIM 26 | How does heat move through solids?

Did you ever grab a hot pan handle? The handle was hot even though it wasn't over the burner. How did the heat move to the handle?

First, the bottom of the pan became hot. The molecules there vibrated faster and faster. As they vibrated, they bumped into other molecules. Then, the other molecules *became hot, vibrated faster,* and *bumped into other molecules.*

This happened over and over again. As it did, the heat moved farther along. Soon, the entire pan was hot.

The passing along of heat from *molecule to molecule* is called *conduction* [kon DUCK shun]. Only solids move heat by conduction.

In solids, the molecules are packed very close together. They cannot move from place to place. The molecules just vibrate faster and faster when a solid is heated.

All solids conduct heat. Some conduct heat much better than others. Solids that conduct heat well are called good *conductors.* Metals are the best heat conductors.

Wood, glass, and plastics do not conduct heat well. They are *poor conductors.* Poor conductors are used as *insulators* [IN soo late erz]. Insulators keep heat from moving where it is not wanted. They keep things from becoming too hot or too cold. If the handle of the pan is covered by an insulator, you won't burn your hand.

Insulators protect us from heat and cold. They keep us comfortable.

WHAT DO THE PICTURES SHOW?

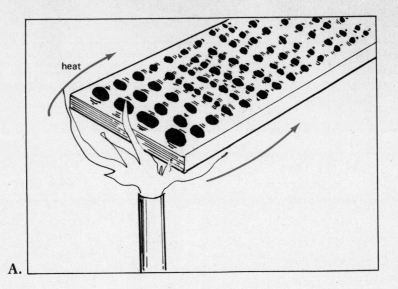

A.

Look at each picture. Then answer the questions for Figures **B** and **C**.

Heat moves through solids by *conduction*.

In conduction, heat is passed along *from molecule to molecule*.

Figure **B** shows six rings of wax on a metal rod. The flame has just been placed under the rod.

B.

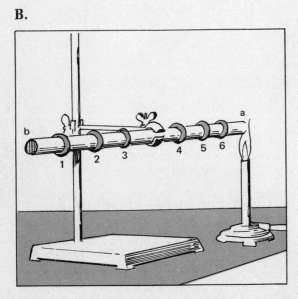

1. Which wax ring will melt first?

   _____

2. Which wax ring will melt last?

   _____

3. Which end gets hot first? _____

4. Which end gets hot last? _____

5. What do we call the way heat moves

   in solids? _____

159

C.

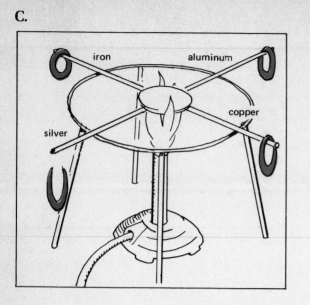

Figure **C** shows wax rings at same distance from flame.

6. Are all the wax rings melting at the same time? _____

7. Are the rods made of the same metal? _____

8. a) Which one of these rods conducts heat best? _____

   b) How do you know?
      a) The wax melts first.
      b) The wax melts last.

   _____

9. a) Which one conducts heat slowest? _____

   b) How do you know?
      a) The wax melts first.   b) The wax melts last.

   _____

10. This experiment shows that conduction is _____ .
    the same for all solids, different for different solids

MATCHING   Match the two lists. Write the correct letter on the line next to each number.

1. _____ insulate   a) good heat conductors

2. _____ metals   b) give off heat energy

3. _____ conduction   c) poor heat conductors

4. _____ plastics and wood d) to protect against heat or cold

5. _____ vibrating molecules e) the way heat moves in solids

COMPLETING SENTENCES

Complete the sentences with the choices below.

insulator	faster	solids
vibrate	metals	heat
conduction	bump	do not
protect	better	

1. Heat makes molecules vibrate _____.

2. The faster molecules vibrate, the more they _____ into other molecules.

3. When molecules hit other molecules, the other molecules _____ faster and give off more _____.

4. The passing of heat from molecule to molecule is called _____.

5. Only _____ move heat by conduction.

6. Molecules of solids _____ move from place to place.

7. The best conductors of heat are _____.

8. Some metals are _____ heat conductors than others.

9. A poor conductor is called an _____.

10. The job of an insulator is to _____ against unwanted heat.

TRUE OR FALSE

Write T on the line next to the number if the sentence is true. Write F if the sentence is false.

1. _____ All matter has heat.

2. _____ Heat can move from place to place.

3. _____ Molecules vibrate slower when they are heated.

4. _____ Heat moves through liquids and gases by conduction.

5. _____ Conduction moves heat from molecule to molecule.

6. _____ In conduction, molecules move from place to place.

7. _____ All solids are good conductors of heat.

8. _____ Metals are good conductors of heat.

9. _____ Metals are good insulators of heat.

10. _____ Wood and plastics are good insulators of heat.

The words in this list are hidden in the groups of letters. Try
to find each word. Draw a line around each word. The spelling
may go in any direction: up-and-down, across, or diagonally.

HEAT
SUN
FRICTION
ENERGY
FUEL
EXPAND
CONTRACT

T	E	N	D	R	H	F
C	X	O	N	E	O	X
A	P	I	A	N	L	A
R	L	T	P	O	E	N
T	S	C	X	N	U	H
N	O	I	E	S	F	L
O	P	R	I	R	T	N
C	G	F	F	I	C	O
Y	G	I	O	L	F	U

**REACHING
OUT** How can you make molecules of metals move from place to
place?

_____

_____

_____

_____

HOW DOES HEAT MOVE THROUGH LIQUIDS AND GASES?

27

convection: the way heat moves through liquids and gases

AIM
27

How does heat move through liquids and gases?

You have learned that the molecules of solids are packed very close together. When a solid is heated, its molecules vibrate faster, but they *cannot* move from place to place.

The molecules of liquids and gases are *not* tightly packed. There are spaces between the molecules. This means that the molecules *can* move from place to place.

What happens when a liquid or gas is heated?

Follow this explanation step-by-step. (Also look at Figure D.)

- The molecules closest to the heat get hot first. They vibrate faster. *They also move.* They move *away from* the heat.

- Cooler molecules move in and take their place.

- The cooler molecules are heated. Then they move away.

- Other molecules move in to take their place.

This happens over and over again. Little by little, all the molecules in the gas or liquid are heated. The molecules that were heated first cool a bit. Then they move back toward the heat and are heated again. This happens over and over— *heating, cooling,* and then *re-heating.*

The passing along of heat by *moving molecules* is called *convection* [kon VECK shun]. Only gases and liquids are heated by convection.

WHAT DO THE DIAGRAMS SHOW?

The diagrams below show atoms of solids, liquids, and gases. Study the diagrams. Then answer the questions below.

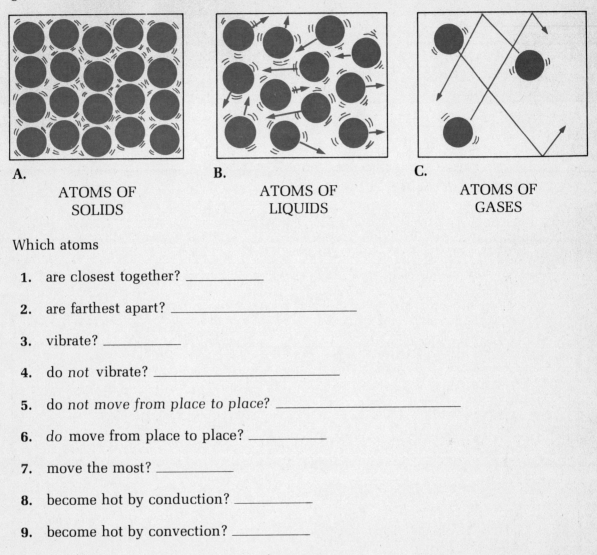

A.
ATOMS OF SOLIDS

B.
ATOMS OF LIQUIDS

C.
ATOMS OF GASES

Which atoms

1. are closest together? _____

2. are farthest apart? _____

3. vibrate? _____

4. do *not* vibrate? _____

5. do *not move from place to place?* _____

6. *do* move from place to place? _____

7. move the most? _____

8. become hot by conduction? _____

9. become hot by convection? _____

STUDYING CONVECTION IN A LIQUID

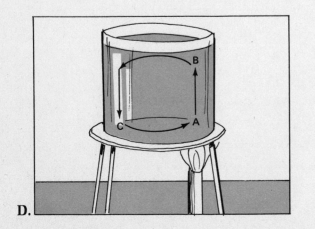

D.

1. The water at A is heated first. It rises to B.

2. As it rises, it cools a bit.

3. The cooled water turns around and drops to C. Then it moves to A again. Here it is reheated.

4. Now, start again with step 1. Repeat the steps over and over and over again.

STUDYING CONVECTION IN GASES

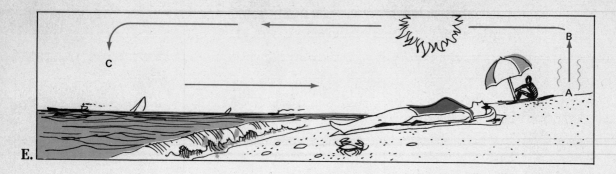

E.

I. **1.** The sun heats the air. The air over the ground, A, becomes warm first. It rises to B.

2. As it rises, it cools.

3. The cooler air turns around and drops to C. It then moves to A again. Here it is reheated.

4. Now start again with step 1. Repeat the steps over and over again.

When air from A rises, other air from C moves in to take its place. What do you call this kind of moving air? _____ (Take a guess. You *know* this term. *You use it often.*)

II. This is called a *convection box*.

The burning candle makes air move out of one chimney and into the other.

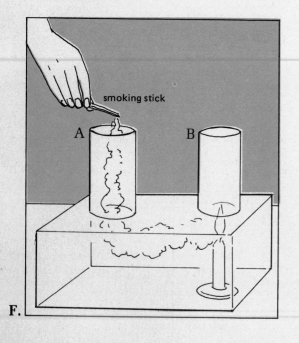

smoking stick

F.

1. Which air is warmer? The air in chimney _____.

A, B

2. Which air is cooler? The air in chimney _____.

A, B

3. Air in chimney B is _____.

rising, falling

4. Air in chimney A is _____.

rising, falling

5. Air is moving from _____.

A to B, B to A

6. Draw arrows to show how the air moves.

166

COMPLETING SENTENCES Complete the sentences with the choices below.

take their place	conduction	gases
convection	more	friction
cannot	solids	vibrating
sun	move away	

1. Molecules of _____ are closest together.

2. Molecules of _____ are farthest apart.

3. Heat moves through solids by a method called _____.

4. Heat moves through liquids and gases by a method called _____.

5. Heat is caused by _____ molecules.

6. The faster molecules vibrate, the _____ heat they give off.

7. In conduction, vibrating molecules _____ move from place to place.

8. In convection, heated molecules _____ and other molecules

   _____.

9. Almost all of our heat energy comes from the _____.

10. Another name for rubbing is _____.

MATCHING Match the two lists. Write the correct letter on the line next to each number.

1. _____ conduction

2. _____ convection

3. _____ solids

4. _____ gases

5. _____ sun

a) molecules farthest apart

b) the way heat moves through solids

c) source of most of our energy

d) the way heat moves through liquids and gases

e) molecules closest together

TRUE OR FALSE   Write T on the line next to the number if the sentence is true. Write F if the sentence is false.

1. _____ Only molecules of solids vibrate.

2. _____ Molecules of solids can move from place to place.

3. _____ Molecules of liquids and gases can move from place to place.

4. _____ Molecules of liquids are closer together than molecules of gases.

5. _____ Molecules of solids are closer together than molecules of liquids.

6. _____ Heat makes molecules vibrate faster.

7. _____ The faster molecules vibrate, the more heat they give off.

8. _____ Cooling makes molecules vibrate faster.

9. _____ All molecules vibrate at the same speed.

10. _____ All our energy comes from the sun.

REACHING OUT   Why should a room have a window open from the top *and* the bottom?

_____

_____

_____

_____

HOW DOES THE SUN'S HEAT REACH US?

28

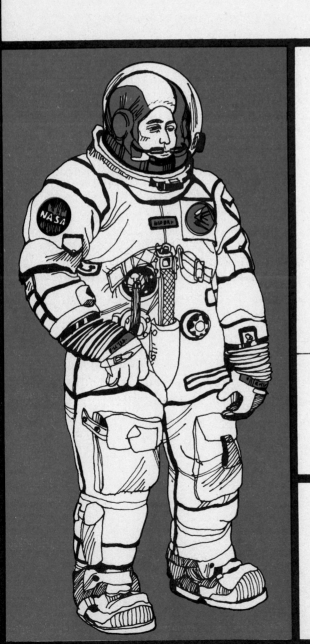

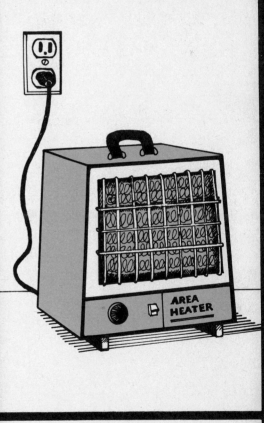

AREA HEATER

radiation: the way heat moves through empty space

reflect: to bounce off

absorb: to take in

AIM 28 | How does the sun's heat reach us?

Can heat move where there is no matter?

You have learned that in conduction and convection, heat is carried by vibrating molecules. And *molecules are matter.*

Most of our heat comes from the sun. And the sun is 150 million kilometers (93 million miles) away. Most of this great distance is *empty space.* There are no molecules there.

Then, how does the heat reach us?

There is a *third* way that heat travels. Heat moves through empty space by *radiation.* Radiation needs no molecules. The sun's heat reaches us by radiation.

When the sun's heat reaches the earth, two things happen.

1. Part of the heat *bounces off* the surface of the earth. It is *reflected.*
2. Part of the heat is *taken in* by the air, water, and land. It is *absorbed.* Matter warms up when it absorbs heat energy.

Radiation does not come only from outer space. Heat from a flame or a hot object reaches us by radiation. We would feel some of the heat even if there were no molecules of air around us.

COLOR AFFECTS HOW MUCH OF THE SUN'S ENERGY AN OBJECT ABSORBS OR REFLECTS

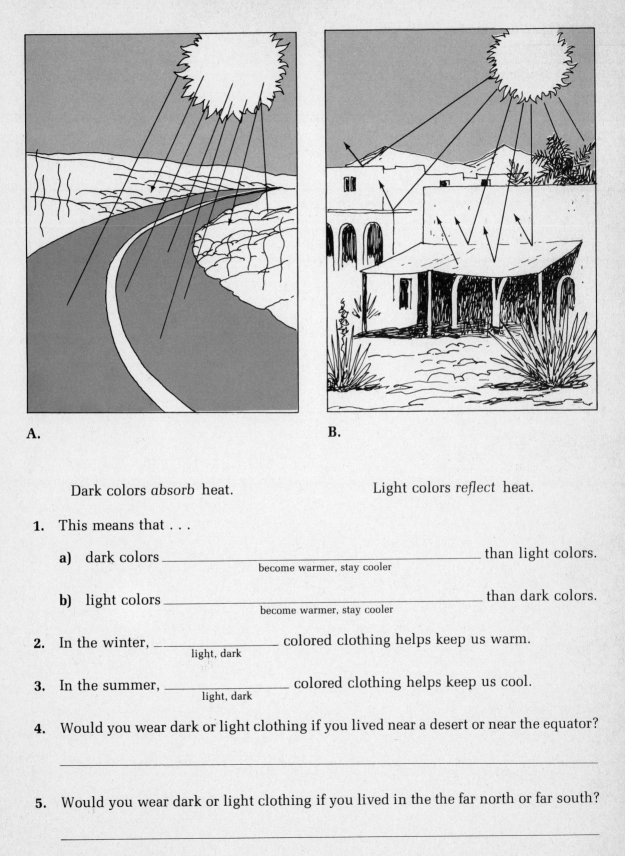

A.

B.

Dark colors *absorb* heat.   Light colors *reflect* heat.

1. This means that . . .

   a) dark colors _____ than light colors.
   <u>become warmer, stay cooler</u>

   b) light colors _____ than dark colors.
   <u>become warmer, stay cooler</u>

2. In the winter, _____ colored clothing helps keep us warm.
   <u>light, dark</u>

3. In the summer, _____ colored clothing helps keep us cool.
   <u>light, dark</u>

4. Would you wear dark or light clothing if you lived near a desert or near the equator?

   _____

5. Would you wear dark or light clothing if you lived in the the far north or far south?

   _____

COMPLETING SENTENCES

Complete the sentences with the choices below. One of these may be used twice.

reflect   conduction   matter
radiation   absorbed   absorb
convection   empty space   reflected

1. Heat moves through solids by a method called _____.

2. Heat moves through liquids and gases by a method called _____.

3. In conduction and convection, heat moves through _____.

4. Between the sun and the earth there is mostly _____.

5. Energy that can move through empty space is called _____.

6. The sun's energy reaches us by a method called _____.

7. Energy that is taken in is "_____".

8. Matter that bounces off is "_____".

9. Dark colors _____ heat.

10. Light colors _____ heat.

THROW ONE OUT!

In each of the following sets of terms, one of the terms does *not* belong. Circle that term.

1. conduction   convection   atmosphere

2. radiation   convection   outer space

3. dark colors   light colors   absorb

4. dark colors   light colors   reflect

5. molecules   conduction   radiation

1. Heat moves through solids by _____.
   <u>conduction, convection, radiation</u>

2. Heat moves through liquids by _____.
   <u>conduction, convection, radiation</u>

3. Heat moves through gases by _____.
   <u>conduction, convection, radiation</u>

4. Heat moves through outer space by _____.
   <u>conduction, convection, radiation</u>

5. Conduction _____ need molecules.
   <u>does, does not</u>

6. Convection _____ need molecules.
   <u>does, does not</u>

7. Radiation _____ need molecules.
   <u>does, does not</u>

8. Heat that reaches the earth is _____.
   <u>absorbed only, reflected only, absorbed and reflected</u>

9. Dark colors mostly _____ heat.
   <u>absorb, reflect</u>

10. Light colors mostly _____ heat.
    <u>absorb, reflect</u>

WORD SCRAMBLE Unscramble each of the following to form a word or term that you have read in this Aim.

1. DAITRONIA _____

2. SCEAP _____

3. BRASBO _____

4. FLERTCE _____

5. MEYPT _____

CONDUCTION, CONVECTION, OR RADIATION?

Fill in each blank space with one or more of these terms.

1. The way heat moves through liquids and gases _____

2. The way heat reaches the moon _____

3. The way heat moves through solids _____

4. Heat-movement that needs *no* molecules _____

5. Heat-movements that *need* molecules _____

_____

MATCHING Match the two lists. Write the correct letter on the line next to each number.

1. _____ conduction and convection

2. _____ radiation

3. _____ dark colors

4. _____ light colors

5. _____ molecules

a) absorb radiation

b) always vibrating

c) need molecules

d) reflect radiation

e) needs no molecules

REACHING OUT How can pollution change the temperature of our planet?

_____

_____

_____

_____

WHAT IS THE DIFFERENCE BETWEEN HEAT AND TEMPERATURE?

29

temperature: the amount of heat we feel

heat: the total amount of energy of a group of molecules

calorie: a unit to measure heat

"What a hot day!"
"Gee! It's cold!"
"What's the temperature outside?"
"Ma! My head feels warm!"

We often talk about heat and temperature. Are they the same? Heat and temperature are *related*. But they are *not* the same.

TEMPERATURE

The word *temperature* is used to describe the amount of heat felt. Temperature is measured with a *thermometer*. Temperature is measured in *degrees*. We use different thermometers to measure the temperatures of our bodies, the temperature outdoors, the temperature of an oven. But the measurement is always in degrees.

Temperature depends on *how fast molecules vibrate*. The faster molecules vibrate, the higher the temperature. The slower they vibrate, the lower the temperature.

HEAT

Heat is the total energy given off by all the vibrating molecules in a bit of matter.

Heat depends on two things: *how fast molecules vibrate (temperature)*, and *how many molecules vibrate*. That means that *size* affects the amount of heat. Larger things have more molecules. So if you have a large object and a small object with the same temperature, the large object will have more heat.

Heat is measured in *calories*. Have you heard that word before?

WHAT DO THE PICTURES SHOW?

Test your understanding of temperature and heat. Study the drawings below. Then answer the questions that go with each diagram.

A.

I. Look at Figure **A.** Both the match and the water are hot. The flame has a higher temperature than boiling water.

1. Can a single match boil this much water? _____

2. Which one do you think can melt more ice? _____
   the burning match, the boiling water

3. Which has more *heat*? _____
   the burning match, the boiling water

4. This shows that higher temperature _____ always mean more heat.
   does, does not

5. The boiling water has more heat because it has _____.
   more molecules, a higher temperature

6. The term that describes the "feeling" of heat is _____.
   calories, temperature

7. The term that describes *total heat energy* is _____.
   calories, temperature

B.   *Both pots contain boiling water.*

II.   Look at Figure **B.**

8.   In comparing *temperatures,*
    a)   a is higher than b
    b)   b is higher than a
    c)   a and b are the same

9.   In comparing the *speed of their vibrating molecules,*
    a)   a vibrates faster than b
    b)   b vibrates faster than a
    c)   a and b vibrate at the same speed

10.   **a)**   a and b _____ have the same *calories.*
                     _{do, do not}

     b)   Which one has *fewer* calories? _____ Why? _____

     c)   Which one has *more* calories? _____ Why? _____

COMPLETING SENTENCES Complete the sentences with the choices below. One of these may be used twice.

less heat
lower temperature
expand
how fast molecules vibrate

degrees
related
higher temperature
calories

not
the number of molecules
more heat

1. Heat and temperature are _____ but they are _____ the same.

2. *Temperature* depends upon _____.

3. *Heat* depends on _____ and also _____ that vibrate.

4. *Faster* vibrating molecules mean _____.

5. *Slower* vibrating molecules mean _____.

6. *More* vibrating molecules usually mean _____.

7. *Fewer* vibrating molecules usually mean _____.

8. Temperature is measured in units called _____.

9. Heat is measured in units called _____.

10. Heat makes matter _____.

TRUE OR FALSE Write T on the line next to the number if the sentence is true. Write F if the sentence is false.

1. _____ Heat comes from vibrating molecules.

2. _____ Molecules always vibrate at the same speed.

3. _____ The faster molecules vibrate, the less heat they give off.

4. _____ Temperature tells us how fast molecules vibrate.

5. _____ Temperature is measured in calories.

6. _____ We measure temperature with a barometer.

7. _____ Heat depends only on how fast molecules vibrate.

8. _____ Ice has heat.

9. _____ An ice cube has the same amount of heat as a block of ice.

10. _____ Heat energy is measured in calories.

MATCHING   Match the two lists. Write the correct letter on the line next to each number.

1. _____ temperature

2. _____ heat

3. _____ degree

4. _____ calorie

5. _____ temperature and heat

a) depends upon how fast and how many molecules vibrate

b) measure of heat

c) related but not the same

d) measure of temperature

e) depends upon how fast molecules vibrate

THROW ONE OUT!   In each of the following sets of terms, one of the terms does *not* belong. Circle that term.

1. friction   sun   source of most heat

2. molecules vibrate faster   temperature rises   temperature drops

3. molecules vibrate slower   temperature rises   temperature drops

4. temperature   degrees   heat

5. heat   calories   degrees

HOW DOES A THERMOMETER WORK?

30

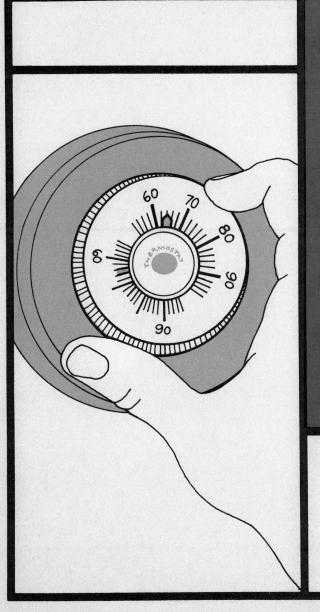

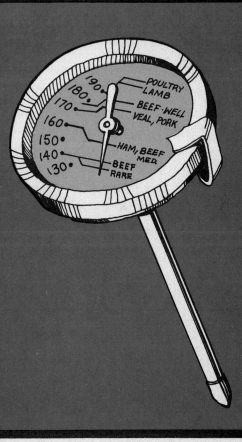

thermometer: instrument that measures temperature

scale: a way of setting up numbers

Fahrenheit: } two kinds of temperature scales
Celsius:

AIM 30 | How does a thermometer work?

Think of all the ways you use thermometers. They tell you indoor temperature and outdoor temperature. A thermometer in meat tells if the meat is cooked well enough. A thermometer in a refrigerator tells whether the refrigerator is cold enough. When you don't feel well, you take your temperature with a thermometer.

No matter what kind of thermometer you use, it works because of two facts you already know:

1. Matter expands when it is heated.
2. Matter contracts when it is cooled.

In most thermometers, the matter that expands or contracts is a liquid. The main part of a thermometer is a long closed tube. At one end the tube gets larger. This end is called the *bulb*. The bulb is filled with a liquid that runs part way up the tube. In most thermometers, the liquid is either *mercury* or *colored alcohol*.

1. When the liquid in a thermometer is heated, it expands. It *rises* in the tube.
2. When the liquid in the thermometer is cooled, it contracts. It *falls* in the tube.

Numbers and lines on the side of the tube tell us the temperature in *degrees*. There are two popular temperature scales. In the United States, the *Fahrenheit* scale is often used. In most of the rest of the world, the *Celsius* scale is used. Scientists everywhere use the Celsius scale. The United States is switching to the Celsius scale. You may as well learn to use it now. You'll need it!

A.

Fahrenheit

I. Look at the thermometer in Figure **A**. Then answer the questions.

1. The *tube* is lettered _____.
   _{a, b}

2. The *bulb* is lettered _____.
   _{a, b}

3. Name two liquids that are used in liquid thermometers.

   _____

4. When heated, the liquid _____ in the tube.
   _{rises, falls}

5. When cooled, the liquid _____ in the tube.
   _{rises, falls}

6. This is a _____ scale thermometer.
   _{Fahrenheit, Celsius}

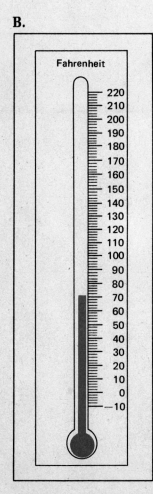

B.

Fahrenheit

II. Look at the thermometer in Figure **B**. Then answer the questions.

The temperature on this Fahrenheit thermometer is *72 degrees*. In symbol form it is written *72°F.*

7. How do you think you write *72 degrees Celsius?* _____

8. In this thermometer, how many degrees does each line

   stand for? _____

9. Take a guess! Do all thermometers have the same number

   of degrees between lines? _____

10. Write the following temperatures in symbol form:

    a) twenty-two degrees Fahrenheit _____.

    b) one hundred degrees Celsius _____.

    c) *minus* five degrees Fahrenheit _____.

    d) seventy-nine degrees Fahrenheit _____.

    e) forty-four degrees Celsius _____.

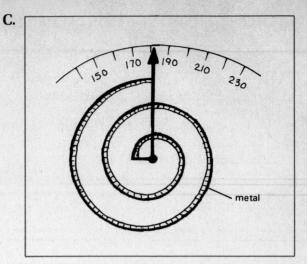

C.

Some thermometers tell temperature because a *metal coil* inside them expands or contracts.

Oven and meat thermometers are examples.

COMPLETING SENTENCES Complete the sentences with the choices below. One of these may be used twice.

---

become smaller	colored alcohol	become bigger
falls	liquid	heated
Fahrenheit	thermometer	mercury
cooled	rises	Celsius

1. We measure temperature with a _____ .

2. A thermometer works because matter expands when _____ and contracts when _____ .

3. There are two main kinds of temperature scales. They are _____ and

   _____ .

4. In the United States the _____ scale has been used most often.

5. In most thermometers, a _____ is used.

6. Two common liquids used in thermometers are _____ and

   _____ .

7. When heated, the liquid _____ in the thermometer tube.

8. When cooled, the liquid _____ in the thermometer tube.

9. Contract means to _____ .

10. Expand means to _____ .

WORKING WITH THERMOMETERS

The diagram below shows a Fahrenheit thermometer and a Celsius thermometer.

See how the scales are different. Study them. Then fill in the temperatures below.

Line up the numbers with a straight edge. Each line stands for two degrees.

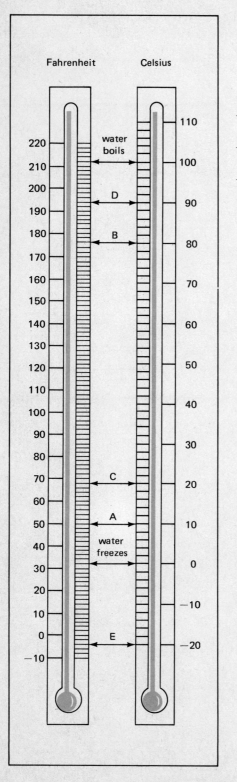

I.		Fahrenheit	Celsius
1.	Water boils		
2.	Water freezes		

II.	Point on Thermometers	Fahrenheit	Celsius
3.	A	50°	
4.	B		80°
5.	C		20°
6.	D	194°	
7.	E	−4°	

8. 86° F is the same temperature as _____ ° C.

9. 104° F is the same temperature as _____ ° C.

10. 50° C is the same temperature as _____ ° F.

11. −10° C is the same temperature as _____ ° F.

12. 40° C is the same temperature as _____ ° F.

13. 60° C is the same temperature as _____ ° F.

14. 158° F is the same temperature as _____ ° C.

15. What temperature would you want it to be all the time?
Write your answer in both Fahrenheit and Celsius. _____ _____

The words in this list are hidden in the groups of letters. Try to find each word. Draw a line around each word. The spelling may go in any direction: up-and-down, across, or diagonally.

LIQUID
CALORIE
VIBRATE
DEGREE
MATTER
ABSORB
REFLECT

B	R	O	S	B	A	Q	L
R	E	T	T	A	M	V	D
Q	F	S	A	P	I	P	E
L	L	T	I	B	S	O	L
D	E	G	R	E	E	L	F
I	C	A	O	L	M	I	E
P	T	D	I	U	Q	I	L
E	I	R	O	L	A	C	R

REACHING OUT

Why is water not used in thermometers?

_____

_____

_____

_____